BY THE EDITORS OF CONSUMER GUIDE®

THE AMERICAN SPORTS CAR

Manufactured in the United States of America
1 2 3 4 5 6 7 8 9 10

Library of Congress Catalog Card Number: 79-87886
ISBN 0-517-289466

This edition published by:
Beekman House
A Division of Crown Publishers, Inc.
One Park Avenue
New York, N.Y. 10016

Cover Photo Credits: Arnolt Bristol coupe and convertible,
owner—Al Morris, photographer—Rich Taylor; 1954 Kaiser
Darrin, owner—Ted Dahlmann, photographer—Bud Juneau;
Mercer T-head Raceabout, owner—Briggs Cunningham
Museum, photographer—Neil Perry; Excalibur J, owner—Brooks
Stevens; Corvette XP-700, Chevrolet Division of General Motors
Corp.; 1957 Ford Thunderbird, Ford Motor Co.

Photo Credits: American Motors Corp.; Brooks Stevens, Brooks
Stevens Automotive Museum; Bud Juneau; Buick Division of
General Motors Corp.; Cadillac Division of General Motors
Corp.; Chevrolet Division of General Motors Corp.; Chrysler
Corp.; Ford Motor Co.; Greenfield Village and Henry Ford
Museum; Henry Austin Clark, Jr.; Oldsmobile Division of
General Motors Corp.; Pontiac Division of General Motors
Corp.; Rich Taylor.
Illustrations: Jeff Lloyd

INTRODUCTION

The scene is Watkins Glen, New York, September 1953—the Grand Prix of the United States. In modified Class D, mainly occupied by expensive foreign iron, industrial designer Brooks Stevens has entered an offbeat challenger. Stevens' two-seater is a little grasshopper of a car, with cycle fenders and a ground-hugging body. Its driver is Hal Ullrich. Three hours later, as the checkered flag greets the winners, Ullrich crosses the finish line first in class. And, to the chagrin of those who came to see Ferrari, Jaguar and Mercedes-Benz racers, Ullrich's car finishes an unbelievable third overall. Its name is Excalibur J—a car based on an unassuming compact built in Willow Run, Michigan. It is as American as a Cadillac Eldorado.

Mention American sports cars, though, and a lot of people immediately don blinders. There is only one worthy of the name, they say—the Chevrolet Corvette. The two-seat Thunderbirds that Ford built for three years in the 1950s really weren't sports cars, they add. And anyway, besides T-bird and Corvette, what was there?

Actually, there was plenty. The Excalibur J is just one example. Between 1945 and the late '60s, American corporations and many gifted amateurs produced a fleet of sports cars to which we can look back with pride.

What do we mean by "sports car?" There are various definitions, most of them falling into two basic categories. Conservatives on the subject say a sports car must be a two-seater, with a removable or collapsible top. Liberals say it can have more than two seats and come in coupe or fastback form as well as convertible. But the essence of the term—and a criterion with which both sides agree—involves the sports car's dual function: it must be capable of normal passenger transportation, yet be easily convertible into a competition car that is able to hold its own on a race track or a road course.

This dual nature has characterized the sports car from the very beginning, when Americans were as familiar with it as were Europeans. In the early 1900s, firms like Simplex, Locomobile and Lozier captured America's imagination with light runabouts that were capable of remarkable performance on road or track. But the two makes that really won our hearts were Stutz and Mercer. Their heyday ran from about 1910 to 1920. That was an age of rakehell ivy leaguers who tore up dusty roads in raccoon-coated merriment; and of dare-devils like Ralph de Palma and Barney Oldfield, who circled dirt tracks at speeds faster than earthlings had a right to go—or so people thought in those years.

Such automobiles fell out of favor in the '20s and '30s, when Americans turned to big luxury tourers like Duesenbergs and Pierce-Arrows. But when GIs began bringing home MGs and Jaguars after World War II, the automotive character of the ancient Stutz and Mercer returned with them. And by then, sports cars were within reach of many besides the idle rich.

American sports cars of 1945 to 1970 are the main subject of this book. They are distinguished from performance cars of the grand touring type, as well as all-out competition machines. GTs like the Studebaker Avanti, Pontiac GTO and Chevrolet Camaro are fast cars of a different class, which played a different role. Sports racing cars like the Chaparral, Scarab, and Ford GT-40 were not true sports cars because they were rarely encountered off the track.

Most of the cars discussed here are two-seaters, and most are convertibles. But there are a few exceptions—notably the Shelby, which could hardly be left out. Carroll Shelby's Mustang-based powerhouse was as genuine a sports car as America ever produced, its coupe bodywork and four seats notwithstanding. This it proved on the track.

Another brand of sports car often overlooked is the exotic specials produced by the big Detroit manufacturers. The Buick LeSabre, Packard Panther, Cadillac Le Mans and Chrysler K-310 thrilled showgoers in the 1950s, and were technically interesting as well. Others like the DeSoto Adventurer and Plymouth XNR came closer to mass production than many people realize.

Important too, in the American sports car story, is the hybrid, a European car with an American engine. Sometimes created through an engine swap on an existing model, sometimes designed from the ground up, hybrids embody all forms from luxury express to hell-for-leather brute. Two of the latter type, the AC Cobra of the 1960s and the V8 Allard of the 1950s, were the fastest cars in the world at the time.

Looking back, which these days is one of the more pleasant directions to look, car fanciers can see that America never produced cars that were more innovative, powerful, and soul-satisfying than it did in the years from 1945 to 1970. We're not producing them now. With the exception of Corvette—and you can get a good argument about its current qualifications—America no longer builds sports cars. A decade of federal legislation has made it impossible. The big manufacturers could rarely justify a two-seater's volume in the best of times. Enthusiastic specialists like Wacky Arnolt, Powel Crosley, Briggs Cunningham and Madman Muntz would not be able to operate today. Their goals would be prohibitively expensive. As for American-engined imports like Morgan, Jensen and Bristol, they're still being built overseas. Their sales in the States have not been high enough to require them to undergo emission and safety alterations. And you think twice before crash-testing a $60,000 Bristol. So American enthusiasts are resorting to used cars, 10 to 25 years old. Happily, there are plenty to choose from.

Nobody will tell you these cars are cheap, though there are still a few bargains left. You can buy many of them for well under the cost of a new Ford LTD. Instead of depreciating, they're appreciating in value. A few years from now, that Kurtis you found for $5,000 might be worth $7,500 if you haven't bent it; the LTD will be a candidate for the junkyard, if it isn't there already. There's hardly a more inflation-proof place to put your money these days than into a collector car. Sports cars are the most collectable of all.

American sports cars also happen to be the most practical of their type. You'll lose your mind before you find a new-old stock cylinder head for a vintage English sports car as commonplace as a Triumph TR-3, for example. There's hardly a car in this book whose equivalent part will cost you as much in time, money and false leads. You can also find a gifted grease monkey, probably as near as the corner gas station, who'll have your exotic-looking Apollo humming like a thoroughbred for what it would cost you to have the plugs and points changed on a Ferrari. He'll be just as good tweaking the innards of a Muntz Jet, or a Thunderbird, or a Kaiser-Darrin. He may hesitate a little over a Shelby or a Corvette fuelie—but there are about 20,000 Shelby and Corvette enthusiasts and a half dozen clubs to which you can turn for guidance. American sports cars are not only fun to drive. They're fun to maintain. Assuming you get one in good condition, your major expenses are behind you.

Advice to Buyers

Where do you look for one of these cars? The local or regional newspaper is the best place to start, as well as the big weekend automotive section of semi-nationals like the *Chicago Tribune* and *The New York Times*. Check the "used car" heading as well as the "antiques and classics" column. We know of a Cunningham C-3 that was listed in the used car section by a middle-aged owner who was more eager to find it a home than to make a fistful of dollars. (It still cost the buyer $7,500, mind you. But he sold it three years later for $12,000.)

The old-car press is the largest source of collector cars, along with a lot of uncollectable dogs. Beware, though, that asking-prices here are attuned to the enthusiast market, and may be very high.

Auctions are best avoided, unless you know what you're doing. Cars sold at auction very often have "reserves"—high minimum prices that the seller won't negotiate. The occasional "bargain" you might find could cost a lot of money to put right. It can be very hard to correctly evaluate a car's condition during its brief appearance in an auction paddock.

Unless you're a mechanical genius, and have your own hydraulic lift, spray booth and upholstery shop, you'll find it best to look for cars in original or "good unrestored" condition. They don't cost as much as restorations. Furthermore, this is a way to lower

chances of your ending up with an unauthentic paint job, interior, or engine. And in this game, authenticity is everything. Restorations to original specification are expensive and time-consuming, and can also put the amount you have invested in the car well ahead of its current value. Unless you're out to fill your basement with a lot of useless trophies, pay a little more for a clean original; skip the cars that are in need of paint, engine work or upholstery.

The three main old car periodicals publishing classified ads are: *Hemmings Motor News* (circulation 165,000), Box 380, Bennington, VT 05201; *Old Cars* newspaper (100,000), Iola, WI 54945; and *Cars & Parts* (75,000), Box 482, Sidney, OH 45367.

Expertise may be obtained from two sources: books, and clubs. *Classic Motorbooks,* Box 2, Osceola, WI 54020, publishes a catalogue of automotive books, parts lists and repair manuals. A stamped, self-addressed envelope sent to any of the hobby periodicals will usually get you the address of the car club devoted to your particular model.

Once you have the car of your dreams, you'll need insurance, license plates and expertise. A happy discovery awaits. If you use the car just occasionally, specialized historic car insurance is available at low rates. Most historic policies allow you to set the car's value (within reason). You pay a premium to protect it up to the stated value. This usually runs between 90 cents and $1.80 per $100 valuation, plus $30 or $40 for liability. Rates can be higher for high-loss models like Corvettes.

Collector license plates, again issued for occasional-use hobby cars, are available in most states. Most often they cost less than regular plates. You might pay $25 for a permanent registration, which will be good for as long as you own the car. The majority of collector plates are still limited to cars over 25 years old, but Maryland, Pennsylvania, Wisconsin, and other states offer them for later-model cars that have been judged "collectible" by the authorities. Most of the cars in this book will qualify on that score. Some collectors avoid special plates, however. They feel that the limited-use restriction outweighs the financial advantage. They register the cars in the normal manner.

Locating and buying a good sports car is not easy, not cheap. But to many lovers of automobiles, the effort and the expense are worthwhile. Since you're reading this book, you probably: (1) already own such a car; or (2) can't stop dreaming of owning one.

You hop in your Nash-Healey as the sun comes up on a dewy New England morning. You drive from Bar Harbor to the Cape along twisty back-country roads, and are disappointed when you find your journey's over. You rev up a fuel-injection '57 Corvette in San Francisco and point it north, running flat-out all night up the California coast. These are the joys of sports cars, cars with performance muscle and instant reflexes. Driving one, you're never bored.

An opportunity to wake up your motoring with a car that demands to be driven, not steered, is a compelling reason to find yourself a sports car.

IN THE BEGINNING:
MERCER

Mercer Automobile Co. , Trenton, New Jersey

You can build a pretty good case for both Mercer and Stutz as America's first generally accepted sports cars. There were others, to be sure—dual-purpose race-and-ride cars—that preceded them. But in the early 1900s, Mercer and Stutz were prominent among the generation of American sports cars that set records and won fame on primitive racing circuits around the country.

The two makes were dissimilar. You might compare the light, spare Mercer Raceabout with the 289 AC Cobra; and the heavy, powerful Stutz Bearcat with the hairiest 427 Corvette. And, like Cobra and Corvette, Mercer and Stutz were great rivals for a time.

The Mercer Automobile Company was founded in May 1909 by Ferdinand and Charles Roebling, prominent Trenton engineers; and Anthony and John Kuser, Trenton manufacturers and businessmen. Although the best-known sporting Mercers had T-head engines, the first models of 1910-11 were L-heads. They were designated Type 30, and introduced in late 1909. Their 25 rated horsepower (about 34 bph) four-cylinder engines had a bore/stroke of 4.25x4.50 inches. The

car's ladder chassis had a 116-inch wheelbase, and was fitted with semi-elliptic leaf springs, a semi-floating rear axle, and a three-speed transmission. The speedster model listed for $1,950. Its most notable styling feature was a rounded cowl that ran between the hood and dashboard—very modern for the period. The speedster was built low to the ground, and handled extremely well. A Mercer won the first time it was raced, powering past quicker opposition during 16 hours of day-and-night competition at the 1909 Delaware Valley Automobile Club race in Trenton. Another Mercer, driven by Washington Roebling, finished second at the Savannah, Georgia, light car race in 1910. The car that placed first in that race was a much heavier and more powerful Marmon. It finished only 11 minutes ahead of Roebling's Mercer.

But the Type 30 speedsters of 1910-11 were soon overshadowed by a Mercer that would write history: the T-head Type 35 raceabout. This immortal automobile was designed by Finley Robertson Porter, a dapper, quiet, brilliant engineer from Stroudsburg, Pennsylvania. Porter was on the Mercer scene only until 1915,

Finley Robertson Porter's immortal 1911 Mercer

but writers have compared him to Bugatti, Porsche and Ferrari—strong praise indeed.

Porter's 300 cubic-inch raceabout engine had a bore/stroke of 4.38x5.00 inches. The Association of Licensed Auto Manufacturers rated it at 30.6 horsepower, but on the dynamometer it registered 58 bhp at 1700 rpm. Every engine had to meet or exceed that standard before it was installed in a chassis. The cylinders were cast in pairs, and the combustion chamber was T-shaped. The construction was superb. Bore grinding, for example, was done to a .001-inch tolerance—far in excess of normal standards of manufacture in 1911. The T-head used two spark plugs per cylinder, but a dashboard switch allowed half the plugs to be bypassed during ordinary roadwork. Twin-spark Bosch magneto ignition was gear-driven from the camshaft. The fuel feed was by air pressure from a gear-driven pump. Fuel ran through annealed copper tubing with silver-soldered joints to twin-jet Fletcher carburetors.

The Mercer raceabout used one of the most advanced transmissions of the day: a three-speed selective shift with forged, oil-tempered steel alloy shaft and gears, splined sliding gear shaft, and ball-bearing shaft running. It was quiet in operation, because the pitch diameter of each gear was checked and ground individually. It was also incredibly easy to shift, despite the lack of anything remotely resembling synchromesh. Double clutching was never necessary. The driver could shift quickly from first to second and from second to third, as drivers can today using a modern three-speed transmission.

The 1911 raceabouts (there were other models, but the raceabout was the sports car) sold for $2,150. They used flywheel-mounted clutches, but in 1912 Mercer shifted to a wet-disc clutch. In 1913-14, all Mercers received a four-speed gearbox. The lower half of the transmission case contained shafts, gears and clutch; the case was split, so these parts could be removed without disturbing the rest of the unit. Shift points for a four-speed Mercer were 15, 25 and 35 mph minimum. Actually, second could stretch to 30, and third to 50 mph. Test drivers have noted that any T-head Mercer raceabout worth its salt could do at least 75 mph—in street-stock trim. That was an astounding performance over 60 years ago.

The Mercer body was a beautiful thing, though there wasn't much to it. A pair of low, tight-fitting bucket seats rested on the frame ahead of a large, cylindrical gas-oil tank; a tool box; and twin spare tires. Ahead of the driver was a big "monocle" windshield. The dashboard was a rudimentary wooden affair, the hood was small, and the front fenders were thin and delicate. Canary yellow was the typical raceabout color, but azure and maroon were also available. The wheelbase was 108 inches, a dimension that remained typical among American sports cars through modern times.

The Mercer chassis was as carefully designed as the engine and body. There was a full floating rear axle, with radius rods, connecting axles and frame to take up driving strain. Semi-elliptic, vanadium alloy steel leaf

IN THE BEGINNING: MERCER

springs were used at each corner. The foot brake acted on the transmission by means of a drum mounted on the drive shaft. An emergency brake operated on the rear wheels. On the road, the foot brake was adequate, but racing drivers soon learned to use the hand brake, too.

Weighing only 2,450 pounds, almost unbelievably light for any brass age sports car, the Mercer raceabout was a natural racing machine. Porter always emphasized that racing improved the breed. "Weaknesses that might resist a long tour, or even years of use, will come to the surface in a day of top speed," he said.

Raceabouts were in the thick of competition almost from the day they first left the factory. The first big win was in February 1911, at the Panama-Pacific Light Car race in San Francisco. The driver, Charles Bigelow, was convinced that he had an Indianapolis winner, and begged Porter to enter the Mercer at Indy. Porter obliged. The raceabout, powered by a 300-cid engine- was pitted against such monsters as Ralph DePalma's 597-cid Simplex, Spencer Wishart's 583-cid Mercedes, and the huge Marmons driven by Joe Dawson and Ray Harroun.

Bigelow and Britisher Hughie Hughes drove the two raceabouts at Indy, in a field of 46 cars. Though most of their rivals were race-prepared, the two Mercers were literally driven in from the street—the classic sports-car tradition. Running flat-out, they averaged 63 mph and finished 12th and 14th. Afterwards, Bigelow and Hughes drove them home, in almost showroom condition. According to race reports, neither car had had its hood opened during the entire 500 miles.

In May 1912, Mercer was back at Indianapolis for another try. Against a field of 24 cars, many of them with double its displacement, a Mercer ran third at 76.3 mph. The company, which rarely exaggerated, called this "one of the most sensational performances in the history of automobiling."

In 1912 DePalma switched from Simplex to Mercer, and began tearing up the circuits. In May he won the 300-cid class at Santa Monica, having driven 150.5 miles in 130 minutes, and set a new class record. DePalma caught a night's sleep, appeared with the same car at Los Angeles the next day, and took three more Class C speedway records. Other drivers followed DePalma's lead. Trenton's own Eddie Pullen won the medium-weight race at Tacoma, Washington; Wishart, fresh from driving Mercedes racers, took the Columbus 200-mile dirt track race; Hughes and Pullen finished 1-2 at the Elgin, Illinois, Aurora Trophy.

The ultimate raceabout was designed in 1913 by DePalma, whom Porter had hired as racing team captain. Deciding that anything a 300-cid Mercer could do, a 445-cid Mercer could do better, DePalma supervised construction of the Type 45. This big-inch model (bore/stroke of 4.8x6.2 inches, and later 4.75x6.33) would do close to 120 mph. At San Antonio late in 1913, DePalma swept three of five races, losing only to a 600-cid Simplex in the unlimited-displacement class.

IN THE BEGINNING: MERCER

DePalma predicted great things from his big-inch Mercer, but he never got the opportunity. Trying to improve his racing team still further, Porter hired Barney Oldfield for 1914. This enraged DePalma. The great Italian driver quit Mercer in protest, vowing to whip Oldfield with his old Mercedes in the upcoming Vanderbilt Cup Race. "If he ever gets that tired old boat fixed I'll run it right off the road," Oldfield told reporters.

The 1914 Vanderbilt was a classic. Four laps from the end of the race, Oldfield and DePalma were the only drivers who mattered. Both seemed capable of winning. Suddenly, DePalma signaled that he would make a pit stop on the next lap. But next time around he just kept going. No one knows whether he'd planned it this way or suddenly changed his mind. Oldfield, expecting DePalma to pull in, brought his car into the pits and lost the race. It's doubtful that Oldfield came in only because of DePalma's signal, though, because his tires were in terrible shape. Oldfield had run 294 miles at 75 mph—a spectacular performance.

The T-head raceabouts changed little in the 1913 and 1914 model years. The 1913s, in addition to four-speed gearboxes, had pump-driven fuel feed instead of exhaust pressure feed. The '14s were not changed in any significant way. Despite Oldfield's loss at the Vanderbilt, 1914 was a banner racing year. Wishart and Caleb Bragg ran well at Indianapolis, dropping out only after minor mechanical trouble occurred. Pullen won five important races, plus the prestigious Grand Prize at Santa Monica, California. But the year ended in sadness. At the Elgin race in August, Wishart locked wheels with another Mercer, careered across the track, ripped out 50 feet of fence posts, and was killed. Following Wishart's death, Mercer officials announced that the company's racing program would be discontinued indefinitely.

Wishart's death was a portent, for the T-head raceabout died with him. In 1915 Mercer fielded a new line of cars, powered by a 22-hp L-head four. Porter had left, and Erik H. Delling, designer of the new engine, had replaced him. Delling's engine was a simple and efficient one, which had a five-main-bearing crankshaft, and a displacement of about 300 cubic inches. In raceabout guise, it was capable of propelling a Mercer at 85 miles per hour, 10 mph faster than a T-head. The problem was that the competition was improving at a faster rate, Stutz in particular. The L-head Mercers simply weren't competitive. Most of the races after 1915 were disappointing for the company.

The L-head was not, however, completely without victories. In an amateur race at Chicago, a driver named W. A. Leet averaged 86.8 mph to win. Pullen raced a special 16-valve, overhead cam L-head at 95.2 mph at Sheepshead Bay, New York. That was the fastest average speed ever recorded by a racing Mercer.

Mercer continued building cars through 1923. Then the company folded, possibly as a result of the unreliable, unpopular overhead-valve six-cylinder engine that had been introduced in 1922. Fewer than 5,000 cars had been built by the company in all its years of operation; never more than 500 per year.

About 130 raceabouts are known to exist today, and they rarely change hands. But among people who appreciate automobiles, they will never be forgotten. They were truly in a class by themselves—built for the driver who drove for the sheer exhilaration of it, pouring on the coals on some deserted back road, reveling in the roar of the cutout. For such drivers there never was, and never will be, anything like a Mercer raceabout.

Mercer racer from 1920

STUTZ

Ideal Motor Car., Indianapolis, Indiana, 1911-13
Stutz Motor Car Co. of America, Indianapolis,
Indiana, 1913-37

Mercer men used to say, "You gotta be nutz to drive a Stutz," but Stutz men had something over Mercer: their favorite car continued a sports-car tradition long after its rival had disappeared.

Stutz was dominated by three successive personality groups: founder Harry C. Stutz—hawk-like and tough; financiers Allen A. Ryan, Charles Schwab, Eugene Thayer, and Carl Schmidlap—businessmen, not engineers; and tycoon Frederic E. Moskovics—genial, polished. Moskovics possessed the best abilities of all his predecessors: the mechanical feel of Stutz and the business acumen of the Ryan group. Thus he produced some of the best Stutzes of all.

Harry Stutz, a talented Pennsylvania Dutch mechanic, founded his company—initially called Ideal Motor Car Co.—in 1911. Previously he had designed the sensational American Underslung of 1905, and served as chief engineer for Marmon from 1905 to 1910. In 1911 he designed the four-cylinder T-head Stutz that finished 11th in the Indianapolis 500, earned for his automobile the tribute, "The Car That Made Good in a Day," and helped convince Harry Stutz that he should go into production.

Racing successes followed in 1912 and 1913, and in 1915 the firm produced what was the most advanced American racing engine up to that time: the four-cylinder overhead-camshaft Stutz-Wisconsin. The power plant developed 131 hp from 296 cubic inches. Its performance and reliability made it the American racing champ in 1915, when three cars—known as "The White Squadron" for their color—were raced. They came in 3-4-7 behind Mercedes and Peugeot in the 1915 Indy 500. After this first outing, Stutzes flattened Mercedes, Peugeot and all American opposition (including Duesenberg). They won at Elgin, Minneapolis, and Sheepshead Bay.

The company then retired from racing, and concentrated on selling its cars to private owners. A Stutz's ability to compete, however, was never in doubt. One Stutz won the Chicago 250 in 1917; another came in second in the 1919 Indy 500. The latter car then was shipped to New Zealand, where against substantial European opposition, it won the New Zealand Motor Cup in 1926, '27 and '28. The car is now in the Southward Museum in that nation's capital, fully restored.

"The White Squadron," racing champs from Stutz

IN THE BEGINNING: STUTZ

The automotive paragon of its age, a 1916 Stutz Bearcat

Harry Stutz cashed in on a splendid racing record. The immortal Bearcat was introduced in 1914 with four- and six-cylinder engines. A sportsman's car based on the Stutz F Series, the Bearcat was a low, short-chassis model, which had oversize brakes and offered superior roadholding and high performance. Celebrated in film and song, the Bearcat was the automotive paragon of its age—the most famous American sports car ever built. It created the Stutz image, which was reflected in substantial sales. The image lives on today.

For 1917 the Series R appeared. Its 16-valve engine had a 3.38x6-inch bore/stroke, and a displacement of 360 cubic inches. The engine produced 80 bhp and

The famous Stutz Bearcat, 1917

could power the car to a top speed of 85 mph. With a new body this Bearcat continued through 1919.

Harry Stutz chose the year 1919 to leave the company and start a rival, the HCS. Vice-president Allen A. Ryan held onto his large block of Stutz stock and remained in control of the company. The firm prospered: more than 4,000 cars were sold in 1920. The Schwab interests took over. Despite the recession of 1921, about 3,000 cars were sold. The Bearcat continued, but total sales for 1922 dropped to 1,028. The year 1922 saw the final form of T-head engine, which then produced 88 bhp at 2800 rpm. The Bearcat, with a 3.00:1 rear axle, could achieve nearly 90 mph. Its price was reduced from $2,925 to $2,750, and left-hand drive was adopted in 1923. But sales continued to slip. The obsolescence of the T-head engine was the main problem.

Ryan left in 1923 to build the Frontenac, hoping to sell it through Stutz dealers. But Schwab's group declined. Instead, they hired Charles Crawford from Cole Motor Car Co. to produce a new six-cylinder Stutz. The first such model was the 268-cid Special Six, priced at $1,995. Only 2,100 units were sold in 1923. The factory had hoped for 10,000. Crawford then produced the 288-cid Speedway Six, which started at $2,650. This car fared worse still, so in 1925 the Special was dropped and all Stutzes were powered by the big six.

Stutz's position continued to worsen in the mid-1920s. Racing activities had nearly ceased two or three years earlier, even though the six took a second in 1925 and won in 1926 at Pikes Peak. Stutz historian Mark Howell notes that the car's sporting image had been abandoned by 1925, and it was competing against such long-established touring cars as Nash, Buick and Studebaker—fierce competition.

Neither the company's management nor its engineering department knew what to do. Crawford "sat with arms folded and no ideas for the future," according to one former executive. It seems likely that Stutz would have expired then and there if Frederic E. Moskovics had not come along.

Sportsman, businessman, and engineer, Moskovics was a remarkable man who had a wide background in both American and European industry. His automotive experience included stints at Franklin, Marmon, Mercedes, Remy Electric, and Continental Tire. He had raced with Frayer Miller. He was a wealthy connoisseur and auto enthusiast.

For some years Moskovics had been evolving a high-performance sports car. It was this design that he sold to the chairman of Stutz, Eugene Thayer. Moskovics also offered to serve as Stutz president for a 10 percent share of the Schwab-Thayer-Schmidlap stock. Desperately in need of a dynamic leader, impressed by Moskovics's background and drive, they accepted him.

The new design, which crystalized around 1922, called for a high-efficiency engine, and a low center of gravity. It used a Timkin "FJ" worm drive to lower car height by half a foot. The engine was a single-overhead-camshaft straight eight. It was designed by Charles R. Greuter, whom Moskovics took into the Stutz engineering department.

Work on the new car began in February 1925, and over $1 million went into its development during the following six months. Incredibly, the new Stutz "Vertical Eight with Safety Chassis" appeared on time at the 1926 New York Automobile Show, where it created a

1952 Bearcat, one of Stutz's last production cars

IN THE BEGINNING: STUTZ

sensation as car of the year. It caused a furor at one show after another across the country. Orders were taken for 2,414 cars—a dollar value of $7,250,000—representing six months' output. From a standstill, Stutz went into full production. The Vertical Eight aroused international interest. Its novel engineering and safety features, its rakish lines, outstanding handling, and good performance were widely admired. It had hydraulic brakes, and a 289-cid, 92-hp engine which gave it a top speed of 75 to 80 mph. Six Brewster body styles appeared in 1926, each priced at $2,995.

In 1927 the engine was enlarged to 298 cid, and a 145-inch wheelbase was added in response to demands from coachbuilders. Weymann fabric bodies were available. Stutz was the only American make to offer them as a production feature. Stutz also re-entered racing: factory cars ran in all but one of the American Automobile Association (AAA) races in 1927, and victory followed every appearance. From this competition evolved the ultimate American sports car of the late 1920s: the Black Hawk speedster. In his choice of the name, Moskovics showed the same flair as Harry Stutz had with his Bearcats.

The Black Hawks were the products of Moskovics and his protégé Frank Lockhart. Moskovics's engineering ability was considerable; Lockhart was youthful and dedicated. Between them, they came up with a speedster that was much faster and more battleworthy than the 1926 models. That year at Atlantic City, only 63 hundredths of a second had separated the winning Stutz and the second-place Auburn. At the same place in 1927, two Stutzes lapped the Auburns within the first 10 miles, and won. Their speed averaged 96 mph. Stutz was AAA champion for 1927. But dark days followed.

Lockhart, with Moskovics's support, had produced a Land Speed Record car—the 16-cylinder, 225-mph Stutz Black Hawk. It ran at Daytona in 1928 on untried tires from an obscure maker. A tire blew out, the car crashed, and Lockhart was killed.

Another big setback for Stutz occurred a thousand miles away. Late in 1926, Charles Kettering of General Motors had boasted that he could drive a Cadillac from Detroit to his home in Dayton, Ohio, much faster than a Rolls-Royce. Much discussion followed among car men regarding American versus European cars. The outcome was a bet between Moskovics and his friend C.T. Weymann (of Weymann body fame). Moskovics wagered $25,000 that a Stutz could beat an Hispano-Suize over 24 hours at Indianapolis. The match race took place in April 1928. A Black Hawk speedster was matched against a Hispano-Suize Boulogne. Valve trouble cost Stutz the race; the contest was stopped in the 18th hour while Hispano had a big lead. The poor performance of that Black Hawk doesn't mean Moskovics had overestimated his car's potential. He believed that, car for car, the Stutz was superior because of its better cornering abilities and high-speed stamina. His car was chosen for the contest by lot from among five cars submitted. The Hispano had been specially selected: it was one of three short-wheelbase, lowered,

specially prepared factory racers, with high compression and high-lift camshaft. It has been shown that the Stutz could have won, but results are the only thing that matters in competition.

The match race didn't contribute to the rehabilitation of Stutz's image, but the Le Mans 24 Hours of 1928 did. Privately entered without factory support, a lone Black Hawk gave the Bentley team the greatest shakeup of its career. W.O. Bentley's jaw dropped as the Stutz took high-speed bends with aplomb. His drivers had to fight to keep up. The race was so close, and the lone leading Bentley was in such poor shape at the finish, that a factory-sponsored racing team probably could have won for Stutz. But after Lockhart's fatal crash, the factory had withdrawn from racing.

For 1929 the straight-eight engine was enlarged to 322 cid to deliver 113 bhp at 3300 rpm. The original three-speed transmission was replaced by a four-speed that included an automatic hill-holder, which prevented the car from rolling backward when declutched on hills. There was a standard line of bodies, including the usual speedsters. Moskovics left the presidency in '29, and was succeeded by E.S. Correll.

The factory experimented with supercharging in 1929. Brisson entered three cars at Le Mans. One had been supercharged, though its blower is believed to have been removed before the race. One Stutz took fifth place. The same year, Britain's *MotorSport* magazine timed an unblown Black Hawk at 98 mph. The editors found its roadholding safe, its acceleration "amazing" (70 mph in third) and its power terrific—"near to flying." Such hyperbole was unexpected from the land of Bentleys. Perhaps the best domestic picture of what it must have been like to drive a Black Hawk in those years has been painted by Don Vorderman: "...the glories of cruising effortlessly at 70 or 80 hour after hour, blasting past all else on the highway, savoring the suspension, steering, braking, engine—an American Thoroughbred."

The magnificient DV-32 engine appeared in 1931. Although this power plant's displacement was identical with that of the 1929 straight eight, the DV-32 was equipped with double-overhead cams and pent-roof combustion chamber; it delivered 150 bhp. In the DV-32 Super Bearcat which had a short 116-inch wheelbase, 100 mph was guaranteed.

Yet the depression was doing Stutz in. The company's last production cars were seen in 1932-33. For several more years Stutzes were merely sold off when possible. The company ceased operation in 1937.

Stutz ranks at the top among American sports cars. For more than two decades—alone in its field during the 1920s—Stutz pursued the dual-purpose race-ride goal with success. It doubled as a luxury car in order to make a living, but Stutz men had racing in their blood. Competition imposes inevitable penalities, of course, and the beautifully balanced Stutz Eight was never quite as successful a straight luxury car as were the Packards, Pierces, or Cadillacs. But this in no way detracts from the race-bred heritage and immortality of "The Car that Made Good in a Day."

AMERICAN SPORTS CARS:

American Motors Corp., Kenosha, Wisconsin

Richard A. Teague is a survivor. He broke into the Detroit styling business with Packard in 1951, just as that firm began to slide downhill. He hung on until the bitter end, though, and created some of the better-looking late Packards. After a stint at Chrysler, Teague went to American Motors, where he's been ever since. He has survived more corporate disasters than perhaps any other top manager. Today, he is vice-president for design.

The reason Teague has lasted so long at AMC is that he's more creative and more innovative than many other stylists. Time and time again he's come up with novel ideas that are not only different, but feasible for production. Whether or not his designs led to better sales, Teague deserves credit for his remarkable efforts.

When Teague first walked into the Rambler studio, the disheartening 1961 American was in its clay model stage. "I'll never forget it," he says. "An English

designer was there with me. We both saw this thing and gasped. 'My God, Dick,' said the Englishman. 'It looks like a ruddy ordnance vehicle!'"

Teague's styling concepts changed the AMC image in short order. As soon as the ugly American had run its course (1961-63), Teague replaced it with a much prettier model. He also smoothed the shape of the larger Rambler, and redesigned the luxury Ambassador. He was responsible for the Marlin fastback of 1965-67, which, though bizarre, represented a design of apparent public appeal. But AMC sales were slow in the mid-1960s, and Teague put a lot of thought into brand-new products. One of these, which appeared in January 1966, was the first AMX show car.

For a company that had advertised, "The only race we're interested in is the human race," the bucket-seated fastback AMX was revolutionary. It had Teague's ideas written all over it. The surfaces were clean and tautly developed; the coupe bodywork

Richard Teague's brilliant, cost-effective AMX

AMERICAN SPORTS CARS: AMX

looked Italian, and fast. But the AMX's most novel feature was its "ramble seat"—another Teague brainstorm. This was an adaptation of the classic rumble seat. It consisted of a flip-up rear window and a pair of contoured flip-back rear seats. Closed up, the AMX was a two-seater; opened, the "ramble seat" allowed two more passengers to ride along in the open air. The first prototype received rave reviews, so in June 1966 American Motors instructed Vignale coachworks in Italy to build a fully operational model.

It took two years for this idea car to evolve into the production AMX. Since the car was basically a two-seater, management felt the market for it was limited. Teague used AMX show-car styling themes in the Javelin—a Mustang rival in the $2,500 price class. Javelin made its debut in late '67 as a '68 model, and was satisfyingly popular.

The Javelin having been approved for production, Teague renewed his campaign for a production AMX. He prevailed, as he usually does, and the new car appeared in February 1968. It didn't have the "ramble seat"—that was too expensive to include. But it was otherwise very close to the '66 prototype. It was also brilliantly cost-effective.

Money has been scarce at American Motors throughout its history, and 1968 was no exception. To reduce costs, Teague cleverly cut 12 inches from the Javelin wheelbase, but retained its width, height and track. This allowed the AMX to use existing tooling, but brought its wheelbase down to 97 inches. Weighing 3,340 pounds, the AMX was comparable in most dimensions to the two-passenger Thunderbirds of 1955-57. Its long Javelin hood gave the truncated coupe body racy proportions, despite its 51.7-inch height.

In styling, the AMX was a statement of nearly pure function. The divided Javelin grille was replaced by a single grid. A crisp "character line" extended from the headlights back to the rear wheel opening, and then back to the tail. The only questionable styling details were twin hood blisters which had false air outlets.

Inside, the layout was based on the Javelin, and was thus more of a compromise. Twin reclining bucket seats were fitted, and the area behind them was carpeted. A massive combination crash pad and instrument panel contained a small tachometer, but the tach was mounted too far over to the left for practicality. Testers considered the cockpit "typically American": the steering wheel was placed too far back for straight-arm driving, and the floor shift was positioned a bit too far forward for easy reach.

The performance of the AMX, however, could not be faulted. The car used an enlarged version of the 343-cid AMC V8. This unit displaced 390 cubic inches (bore/stroke 4.17 x 3.57 inches) and had a tall 10.2:1 compression ratio. It produced 315 bhp (gross) at 4500 rpm, with 425 foot-pounds of torque at 3200 rpm. A 390 AMX would accelerate from 0 to 60 mph in little over 7 seconds, and turn the quarter mile in 15.2 seconds at 90 mph. This was impressive performance—certainly the best ever offered by a company known for its Ramblers.

Production engineers have occasionally caused headaches for Teague by watering down his concepts.

The AMX/2, a nonoperational exercise in design

But they cooperated fully with him on the AMX. The car was as sporty as AMC could make it. Standard equipment included a Warner T-10 four-speed gearbox (automatic was optional), dual exhausts, heavy-duty suspension, mag-style wheel discs and E70-14 wide profile tires. The car tracked evenly through turns, and went like a bullet in the straights. Equipped with the optional 3.54:1 rear axle ratio, an AMX would go 110 mph; the standard 3.15:1 ratio would take it to 120. All this added up to a tremendously satisfying package. And the price, with all the above items standard, was only $3,500.

There was some initial contention about whether the AMX was really a sports car. Craig Breedlove silenced the arguments. Breedlove, who then held the world's Land Speed Record, set 106 speed records with the AMX in 1968. The cars were also competitive in road racing. The AMX may have been "typically American," but it was also a true dual-purpose sports car.

American Motors sold 6,725 AMXs for model year 1968, a fraction of the 56,000 Javelin sales. But the firm pressed on with its two-seater. The 1969 AMX was basically unchanged from the year before, though leather upholstery was optional. Racing stripes, part of an optional "go" package, were also available. A few 1969s were painted to match their image: "Big Bad" orange, blue and green. Production for 1969 inched up to 8,293 units.

The AMX inspired two significant mid-engine show cars in the late 1960s. The AMX/2 was a nonoperational design exercise, with a 105-inch wheelbase and independent rear suspension. It led to the wild AMX/3, designed with the help of Bizzarrini and BMW. This was a sleek sports racer with a 340-bhp engine, independent suspension all around, and a top speed of 160 mph. Although its potential was never proved on international racing circuits, its styling did influence the swoopy-looking AMC Matador hardtop.

The last year for the production AMX was 1970. In some ways it was the best year of all. The original coupe body was retained, but styling was new from the cowl forward. The grille was aggressively pointed, and the previous twin hood bulges were replaced by a forward-mounted "power blister." The '70 AMX was two inches longer than the '69 as a result of its front-end revision. The standard engine was a 360-cid V8 which developed 245 bhp; the 390, providing 325 bhp, was optional. The car had a new safety windshield, whose inner laminated panel shattered into tiny blunt particles upon impact to minimize the chance of injury in a crash. Fiberglass-belted tires, high-back bucket seats, energy-absorbing steering column and a horn control running the full circumference of the steering wheel were all standard equipment.

Production in 1970 dropped to 4,116 units for a three-year total of 19,134 AMXs. The model was dropped for a variety of reasons: low sales, AMC's decision to emphasize the Javelin, and the advent of stricter federal safety and emissions regulations. Today, the AMX is a rapidly appreciating collector's item, but you can still find a good one for $2,500 or so. Low production and high performance assures the AMX of continued appreciation. It's hard to think of a better buy among American production sports cars.

The last production model AMX

APOLLO

International Motor Cars, Inc., Oakland, California

Fifteen years ago we were wringing untold horsepower out of small, light, efficient V8 engines like Ford's 260/289, Chevy's 254/283, and Buick's 215. Imaginative people were installing those engines in light, tautly sprung chassis, and wrapping them in exotic bodywork. The result was a new breed of limited-edition gran turismos. The Apollo was one of these automobiles.

Newt Davis and Milt Brown, a pair of enthusiastic entrepreneurs from Oakland, California, conceived the Apollo. They formed a company, designed a chassis, bought a batch of 215.2-cid Buick aluminum V8s, and planned a sleek fastback body. Apollo's somewhat dated styling was created by designer Ron Plescia, with modifications by Franco Scaglione of Turin, Italy. Frank Reisner of Carrozzeria Intermecannica, also of Turin, contracted to build the Apollo bodies.

Apollos were assembled in Oakland. The cars were built painstakingly at a rate of four a month. The paint job, for example, comprised 13 steps and took three weeks to complete. But despite low production and hand assembly, the finished car listed for only $6,597.

The Apollo chassis was designed by Brown. It combined a ladder-type tubular steel frame with a beefed-up Buick Special suspension. The Buick-style drum brakes were not up to the car's performance, although they had special linings. Bendix disc brakes were offered later as an option. A three-speed manual gearbox was standard, but Borg-Warner's T-10 four-speed and Buick's Turbo automatic were available.

Since the Apollo GT weighed only 2,400 pounds, the unmodified Buick V8 (200 horsepower, 240 foot pounds of torque) provided ample performance. A 0-60 sprint took just 8 seconds, and Apollos would run the standing quarter-mile in 16 seconds at 85 mph. The car's handling was comparable with that of Apollo's rivals—Jaguar, Corvette, and Aston Martin. It was less a dual-purpose sports car than, say, the MG, but it wasn't around long enough to really be tested in competition.

International Motor Cars soon added an Apollo cabriolet at $7,347. In 1964, it brought out an additional series, the 5000 GT, which used Buick's 300-cid, 250-hp V8. The 5000 could run 0-60 in 7.5 seconds and had a claimed top speed of over 150 mph.

Davis and Brown were serious about their project, and intent on offering good value for the dollar. But their company had fallen apart by 1966. International soon learned that there was more to building a successful car than careful construction. The Apollo was never advertised nationally, and the firm lacked a sufficient dealer network. The operation was also sidetracked at one point by the distress-sale of a score of Apollo bodies to a Dallas firm, which assembled them under the name Vetta Ventura. International Motors was renamed Apollo International in 1965, and was moved from Oakland to Pasadena. This was a last-ditch recapitalization effort.

Total Apollo production was about 90 cars—the exact figure is unknown.

A 1964 Apollo-one of about 90 built

ARNOLT

S.H. Arnolt, Inc., Chicago, Illinois

The Arnolt-Bristol is a 20-year-old sports car that you might take for a brand-new model if you were to see one right now—except for those delicate bumpers. The car was a landmark design by Nuccio Bertone, one of Italy's great modern coachbuilders. The chassis was built by Bristol of England; the engine was Bristol-derived from the prewar BMW. Yet it is an American sports car because it was conceived and sold by an American, the irrepressible Stanley H. "Wacky" Arnolt.

Wacky Arnolt was a big, garrulous, fun-loving sportsman from Warsaw, Indiana, who first made money by building marine engines during World War II. After the war, he expanded into allied industries. Because he liked automobiles, one of his early interests was a foreign-car dealership in Chicago. By the mid-1950s he was the Midwestern distributor for British Motor Corp., Velo-Solex mopeds, and Solex carburetors. In those days British cars reigned supreme over all other imported automobiles in the United States, so Arnolt went to England each year to see what he could see.

His first creation was the Arnolt-MG, of which 65 were built. Arnolt had found a svelte Bertone body at the Turin Auto Show in 1952; he contracted to buy 100 copies, and went to MG for their innards. The $3,195 Arnolt-MG resembled concurrent MG sports cars only in its narrow, upright grille. The rest was pure Bertone—smooth, sleek, structurally correct. But the MG engine made the car underpowered, to put it charitably. Arnolt wanted something faster, so he turned to Bristol Cars for an engine and chassis.

At that time, Bristol was building a beautiful grand tourer, the 404, which cost $10,000. Arnolt loved the 404, and imported a few. But he wanted a cheaper sports car which he would be able to sell in greater numbers. Bristol sales manager James Watt offered to supply an "economy" 404 chassis. Mainly, this meant 11-inch unfinned drum brakes instead of the 12-inch Lockheed A1-Fin brakes the 404 used. But the cheaper chassis still used the 404's sturdy box-section frame, transverse-leaf independent front suspension, and carefully located live rear axle. The wheelbase was 96 inches—ideal for the car Arnolt planned.

Arnolt also picked up a hotter engine—Bristol's BS1 Mark II. This 220.3-cid four (bore/stroke 2.59x3.77 inches) developed 130 horsepower, against only 105 in the stock 404. Using the light body Arnolt wanted, the new car appeared able to run circles around the Bristol.

The engine was a curious affair. Horizontal pushrods ran across its head—it was very tall. Bertone, to whom Arnolt turned for body styling, had to build the car around it. But some of the best designs seem to come from impossible assignments, and the Arnolt-Bristol was superb. It was unquestionably one of the purest shapes ever to be carried on four wheels.

Bertone started with a low, oval grille cavity for the headlights and air intake. From there the bodywork sloped upward to a rounded hood, and was capped

1955 Arnolt-Bristol roadster

Front view of Arnolt coupe

RICH TAYLOR

17

RICH TAYLOR

Rear view of Arnolt roadster

with an air scoop (more for extra height than for extra air). The hood fell away at the sides, but the fenders rose again, peaking in a sharp crease. The crease swept back along the beltline, and aft to the rear fenders. A secondary crease followed the contour along the body sides. The tail fell off quickly from the rear wheels back. The result was nearly perfect 49-51 weight distribution.

The Arnolt-Bristol was offered in three distinct models. The Bolide—originally priced at $3,995, and later at $4,250—was topless, designed for sunny days or race tracks. A Deluxe model—first $4,765; then $4,995 — had a top, but didn't look half as nice. A coupe was offered at $5,995, with roll-up windows and a luxurious interior.

The Arnolt-Bristol weighed only 2,100 pounds, and went like a comet. Typical performance figures were: 0-60 mph in 8.7 seconds, 0-90 in 21.3 seconds; standing quarter mile in 17 seconds at 82 mph; top speed 110 mph. Its handling and responsiveness were equal to its performance. The rack-and-pinion steering was positive and quick; the car tracked evenly through corners with a trace of final oversteer. Although the brakes were not impressive to look at, no tester was able to provoke serious fade. One magazine even called them "brakes to race with."

And race the Arnolt-Bristol did. In 1955 and 1956, Arnolt entered three cars in the Sebring 12 Hours. Each year they finished 1-2-4 in the two-liter production

category. Interestingly, they were all street-stock: they had not been modified for the races. So the Arnolt-Bristol was as near to the ideal dual-purpose sports car as any vehicle ever built.

Alas, Sebring '57 was one race too many. One of Arnolt's drivers, blinded by the setting sun, rolled his car and was killed instantly. Arnolt took the crash hard, blaming himself. The A-Bs came back to Sebring one more time, in 1960. Three cars with all-aluminum bodies were entered, won the team prize and the two-liter GT class trophy. But Arnolt never raced his cars again. When he died of a heart attack in 1963, the Arnolt-Bristol died with him.

A-B production totaled 142, of which 12 were lost in a warehouse fire. Of the 130 sold, only three were coupes. Five cars had aluminum bodies and large fuel tanks for long-haul racing. Four A-Bs were fitted with 283 Corvette engines, and one had a 100 D2 AC-Bristol engine. About 100 have been located by the Arnolt-Bristol Register.

Arnolt-Bristols were inexpensive because Wacky Arnolt lost a bundle on every one he sold. To make money, he should have charged $6,000 or $7,000. That's about the lowest you can pay for one today; $8,000 or more may be necessary to land a good one. On the plus side, Arnolt's son still has body parts, and Bristol supplies engine spares. If you're fortunate enough to find one, there's no reason to hesitate. The Arnolt-Bristol can hold its own in the best of company.

CORVETTE

**Chevrolet Division of General Motors Corp.,
Detroit, Michigan**

Even in big corporations, notable cars are usually the product of gifted individuals. For America's best-known, highest-selling, longest-lived sports car, we can credit four men in particular. Corvette styling was directed by Harley Earl through the 1960 models, and by William L. Mitchell from 1961 onward. Engineering was the work of Ed Cole in the beginning. Zora Arkus-Duntov set the engineering standards from 1956 almost up to the present. Of course there were scores of others without whom the Corvette as we know it couldn't have existed. Precepts laid down by Earl, Mitchell, Cole and Duntov have guided Corvette development for the car's 25-year life. Their efforts have resulted in a series of memorable sports cars, and sales that were really notable—even for GM.

"To lengthen and lower the American automobile, at times in reality and always at least in practice," was how Earl summed up his 31 years at General Motors. He arrived there in 1927, on an unbeatable recommendation, the 1927 LaSalle. Earl soon set up the GM Art & Colour Studio—the first design department in the automobile industry.

Cole was born in Marne, Michigan, in 1909. In 1930 he enrolled at the GM institute in Flint. He was involved in Cadillac engineering projects before he was graduated. Cole became Cadillac's chief engineer in 1945 and played a decisive role in the development of its revolutionary 1949 V8 engine. In 1952 he was named chief engineer of Chevrolet—a job he had asked for in preference to manufacturing manager. Immediately, Cole quadrupled the engineering staff and began work on what became the Chevrolet 265 V8 engine of 1955—it was the definitive low-displacement, high-performance V8. In the meantime he moved to improve Chevrolet's 235-cid "Blue Flame" six. He raised it from 105 horsepower to 150 in the first Corvette.

GM's sports-car project began in early 1952, with two separate initiatives. The first was a standard Chevy convertible with a body made of glass-reinforced plastic—a new body material of interest to GM body engineers. Simultaneously, a young engineer named Bob McClean designed a chassis, starting from the rear instead of the front. He placed the seats immediately ahead of a solid rear axle, moved the engine and

1953 Motorama Corvette

AMERICAN SPORTS CARS: CORVETTE

transmission as far back as he could, and lowered the drive train. Seeking ideal 50/50 weight distribution, he chose a 102-inch wheelbase, identical with that of the Jaguar XK-120. For the first time in Chevrolet history an open or Hotchkiss drive was used instead of torque-tube drive. Normal leaf springs located the axle, but unlike Chevy cars they were outboard of the main frame rails for added stability.

To raise the 235-cid six to 150 horsepower, Cole designed a high-lift, long-duration cam. He replaced hydraulic valve lifters with solid lifters, and used dual valve springs. A modified cylinder head provided 8:1 compression. The water pump capacity was increased, and a larger radiator fan was fitted. Cole devised a special aluminum intake manifold with three Carter side draft carburetors; each carb fed two cylinders. Cole didn't feel Chevrolet's manual transmission was up to the new engine's 150 horsepower. Since time was short, a Powerglide two-speed automatic was fitted as standard equipment.

While engineers labored with engine and drive train, Harley Earl completed the prototype for the 1953 GM Motorama. Excepting Cowl-mounted fresh-air scoops, the Polo White Motorama Corvette closely prefigured the production 1953 models. There were many detail differences, but the basic car that wowed showgoers in 1953 was much like the Corvette that would later be sold at Chevy dealerships.

The first production cars rolled off a small assembly line in Flint on June 30, 1953—the first of 300 Corvettes for '53. Their frames were purchased from an outside supplier; their engines were produced at the Chevy engine plant in Tonawanda, New York; their fiberglass bodies were built by Molded Fiber Glass Co. in Ashtabula, Ohio. (Assembly shifted to St. Louis, Missouri, in mid-1954.) The '53s were essentially handmade, and were more a market test than a serious production effort. They were rare in 1953, and are the most sought-after Corvettes today. They currently sell for phenomenal prices—up to $30,000 a copy.

Although purists condemned the Corvette for its automatic transmission and fake knock-off wheel covers, it was actually quite a good car. It would do 0-60 mph in about 11 seconds and hit a top speed of 105 mph. As *Motor Trend* put it, "Chevrolet has produced a bucket-seat roadster that will hold its own with Europe's best, short of actual competition and a few imports that cost three times as much."

For the 1954 model year, Chevy built 3,640 Corvettes. For the first time, the cars were available in colors other than Polo White, the standard color on '53s. There were also cars in Pennant blue, Sportsman red, and black. Although the '54s were more of an assembly-line product than the '53s, changes were few. The exhaust extensions were lengthened and vented out the bottom of the car instead of inboard of the rear fenders. After 300 were built, the trunk handle hood release was changed; after car number 1900, the triple chrome air cleaners were replaced by a twin-pot type. A new cam appeared in later engines, raising

horsepower to 155. Some 20 percent of the '54s had chrome-plated rocker covers and ignition shielding.

Sales of the '54 Corvette were disappointing. Analysts suggested that the car was neither fish nor fowl: not an all-out sports car; not a boulevard tourer. At the end of the year, the only year when Corvette failed to sell out, 1,500 models were still unsold. Production of a '55 model was in doubt for awhile, but then the V8 engine arrived, and a new kind of Corvette was born.

The V8 '55 Corvette was so popular that less than 10 six-cylinder models were sold in their last year. The engine produced 195 horsepower at 5000 rpm from the 265-cid (bore/stroke 3.75x3.00) engine. This gave the car a 0-60 time of 8.5 to 9 seconds and raised its top speed proportionally. More important, it made the Corvette faster than the new two-seat Thunderbird—good news at General Motors.

Generally, 1955 bodies were smoother and slightly thinner in section—and better-built than their predecessors. Detail changes included a higher-calibrated 6000 rpm tachometer on the V8 models, and a 12-volt electrical system. The '55 Powerglide transmission was similar to the 1954 version, but a new close-ratio three-speed manual gearbox was installed on a few '55s. Aside from color changes, the only exterior modification was a gold "V" overlaid on the letter "V" in the Chevrolet side script, to identify V8 models.

Unfortunately, 1955 also proved disappointing. Production ended with only 700 units, marking the end of the first Corvette generation. Again, Chevrolet considered the wisdom of building a sports car. The 1956 model convinced corporate managers that they should continue.

The 1956 Corvette was one of the last GM production cars styled in Detroit, before the design department was moved to the Technical Center in Warren, Michigan. Its roots lay in 1955's show cars, the Chevy Biscayne and the LaSalle II. The Biscayne was a four-door hardtop with a vertical-bar grille; the LaSalle II appeared as a sedan and roadster. Both show cars featured concave sections in the body sides, which swept back from the front wheel wells. This was inspired by the classic era's "LaBaron sweep." It was a feature of the 1956 Corvette, and its successors through 1962.

The production shape was beautifully executed. It curved in the right places; its contours looked smooth and purposeful. In a styling sense, it and its look-alike '57 successor were the most beautiful Corvettes of the pre-1963 period. In addition to good looks, it offered improvements on the passenger compartment: roll-up windows, better visibility, and an optional hardtop. The 165 V8 engine was used again, after Duntov modified it. He raised the mill's horsepower to 225 at 5200 rpm with a 9.25:1 compression ratio and a special high-lift cam. Equipped with a manual gearbox and the standard 3.55:1 rear axle ratio, the '56 would turn 0-60 in 7.5 seconds and run the standing quarter mile in 16 seconds at 90 mph. It was capable of almost 120 mph off the showroom floor. As America's only volume

1956 Corvette, C-production SCCA champ

1957 Corvette, basis of the 1963 Sting Ray

sports car, Corvette had reached maturity.

There's no better proof of the '56's worth than its racing record. In 1953-55, Corvettes were of no account on race tracks, but the "Duntov cam" and suspension modifications changed all that. Using a special 250-hp '56, Duntov enabled the Corvette to top 150 mph at Daytona Beach. Then racer John Fitch entered a team of Corvettes in the Sebring 12 Hours. Three were production cars that used the Duntov cam, two four-barrel carbs, and ported manifolds. One was bored to 307 cubic inches and fitted with a four-speed Z-F transmission for the prototype class. The top two Corvettes finished ninth and 15th overall: "less than we had hoped, but more than we deserved," Fitch said. Corvette did better in Sports Car Club of America racing. A car driven by Richard Thompson, a dentist from Washington, D.C., became the C-production SCCA champion in 1956. It was the first of many Thompson winners.

Duntov began building a Sebring SS Corvette in July 1956. This was a sports racer with a tubular space frame, fuel-injected V8, magnesium body, and De Dion rear axle. This car was not successful in its initial runs, and further efforts were stopped by the 1957 Auto Manufacturers Association decision to de-emphasize racing. But Bill Mitchell rescued the SS chassis and reworked it into his own Sting Ray Special. This car was raced in 1959-60 by Thompson and was the

SCCA C-modified champion in '60. It also formed the basis of the Sting Ray design for 1963.

On the surface, the '57 Corvette looked the same as the '56, but many improvements had been made under the skin. There was a new 283 cubic-inch V8 engine, a new optional four-speed gearbox, and optional fuel injection providing 283 hp—one horsepower per cubic inch. Although only 240 fuel-injected models were produced, their performance was an industry byword; in good tune, a "fulie" would leap to 60 in 6.5 seconds.

The 283-cid V8 was produced by boring the 265 one-eighth of an inch to 3.875 inches. The 283 offered higher compression, a higher-lift cam, and a choice of horsepower from 220 to 283. Valve lifters were hydraulic, except on fuel-injected engines, which used mechanical lifters. The four-speed gearbox was built by Borg-Warner to Chevrolet specifications. It cost buyers $188 extra and was worth it. The ratios were set close at 2.20:1, 1.66:1, 1.31:1, and 1:1. Coupled to a fuelie engine and the optional 4.11 rear axle ratio, the car could reduce its 0-60 time to 5.7 seconds and 0-100 to 16.8 seconds.

Chevrolet also took a hard look at the 1957 suspension. An important option was RPO 684, a comprehensive handling package which included front anti-sway bar, heavier springs, stronger shocks, ceramic-metallic brake linings, finned brake drums, quick-steering and "Positraction" limited-slip differential. Two

1958 Corvette SS

Faddish '58 with quad headlights

'59 version similar to its predecessor

1961 Corvette with busy-looking sides

'62 model used less chrome

production models finished 12th and 15th at the Sebring 12 Hours. They were the first GT-class cars to cross the finish line. The lead 'Vette was 20 laps ahead of the nearest Mercedes-Benz 300SL! General Motors went along with the Auto Manufacturers Association's decision to play down racing in car advertising, and did not sponsor competition after 1957. Yet Corvettes continued to run and win, and dominated the SCCA B-production class in 1958 and 1959.

Production in 1956 of 3,467 units, and in 1957 of 6,339 firmly justified the continuance of the Corvette. But 10,000 sales were necessary to make a profit, and GM spent a great deal of time considering how to increase the car's appeal in showrooms. As a result, the '58 adopted faddish quad headlights, and it gained weight. More chrome appeared, and the body grew about 10 inches longer and three inches wider.

Other changes continued to improve the breed. Duntov grouped the instruments under the steering wheel, and the tach became easier to read. The passenger was given a useful (sometimes necessary) grab bar. Fuel injection was made more reliable. The new fuel-injected engine delivered up to 290 bhp at 6200 rpm; carbureted 283s ranged from 230 to 270 bhp.

For 1959 and 1960, styling was manifestly the same as in 1958. Duntov, however, saw to the removal of the fake louvers from the hood, and the relocation of the inside door knobs. The heavy-duty suspension option was continued, and spring settings were made even harder. Sintered metallic brake linings, which cost only $27 and were well worth it, were added. Radius rods were fitted to the rear suspension to reduce axle tramp.

The 1960 Corvette used an increased amount of aluminum—in the clutch housing, radiators, and cylinder heads. But the aluminum heads suffered internal flaws, and tended to warp if the engine ran hot. They were soon dropped. Double sway bars (front and rear) were used instead of the stiff springs. They greatly improved ride and handling. The 1960 Corvette reached a racing milestone at Le Mans. In the 24-hour classic, a three-car team led by Briggs Cunningham ran well in the big-engined GT class. One car driven by Bob Grossman and John Fitch finished eighth, attaining over 151 mph on the Mulsanne Straight.

Development of the 283-cid V8 continued through 1961, its last year of use in the Corvette. Between 1958 and 1961, carbureted versions ranged from 230 to 270 horsepower; fuel-injection units delivered 250 to 315 horsepower.

Mitchell replaced Earl, who retired, in December 1958. The effects of this change were not visible until the 1961 models. The first car Mitchell created that influenced the 1961 restyle was the XP-700. This was basically a stock '58 Corvette, dramatically restyled. The front end was on the weird side: big, wide fenders housed quad headlights and a small oval grille. The sides of the car were very busy. The XP-700 did have a neat rear design, however. The trunk lid was flat, and an accent line rose from the top of the rear wheel wells. These features and the XP-700's recessed taillights

Corvette show car, the XP-700

were adopted on 1961 production Corvettes. The 1961 Corvettes were also influenced by Mitchell's earlier Sting Ray racing car—though the racer more greatly influenced later Corvettes.

In 1962, Mitchell de-emphasized the concave side molding by eliminating its chrome outline. He also replaced the small teeth inside the body side scoop with a simple grid, blacked out the grille, and added ribbed anodized aluminum trim to the rocker panels.

Corvette prices rose considerably between 1956 and 1962. The car listed at only $3,149 in 1956; it jumped to $3,631 in 1958, $3,872 in 1960, and $4,038 in 1962. Fuel-injected models cost over $5,000, some $1,500 more than buyers paid for the first Corvettes in 1953. But the cars of the early 1960s were far different from the 1953-54s, and offered more performance and style for the money.

These '60s Corvettes continued to add to the racing record. Delmo Johnson and Dale Morgan won the GT class at Sebring in 1961. Also in '61, Dick Thompson won the B-production national championship. Don Yenko won it in 1962-63 after Thompson switched to an A-production car with the new 327 cubic-inch V8. Thompson won his fifth national championship in this car, then partially retired. Frank Dominiani was B-production champ in 1964, the last Corvette championship for a long time. After that, Corvettes were outclassed in production racing. The problem was Carroll Shelby's red-hot Cobra. Basically an English AC Ace running a hefty Ford V8, the Cobra lacked Corvette's sales appeal, but it was murder on the race tracks. During the Cobra's lifespan, 1964-67, the Corvettes had trouble keeping up.

One problem Corvettes didn't have was low sales. Production was 10,939 units in 1961. It zoomed up to 14,531 for 1962. The car had become profitable by 1958, but in 1962 it returned real profit on investment.

An important new engine arrived in 1962; the 327-cid V8 (bore/stroke 4.00 x 3.25 inches). This formed the basis for Corvette power through 1965. In 1962-63, it was available with up to 340 hp with carburetors; 360 bhp with fuel injection. Typically, a 327 with the 3.70 rear axle ratio would run the quarter mile in 15 seconds at over 100 mph.

With the 1962 models, the third Corvette generation (1958-62) reached a performance peak. Whatever had remained of its plebian origins was long gone. The '62 Corvettes were not only fast, but good-handling and comfortable as well. Thanks to Mitchell, the styling clichés of 1958-60 had been erased. Thanks to racers like Thompson and enthusiastic engineers like Duntov, Corvette had scored impressively in production racing.

The Corvette Sting Ray of 1963 was a design revolution. Although the 1953-62 'Vette had received many evolutionary changes, none really altered its basic design. The X-braced frame and basic fiberglass body panels were unchanged except in detail from

1963 Sting Ray Sport Coupe

Corvette Sting Ray racer, 1961

The '63 Sting Ray convertible

1953 through 1962. The Sting Ray marked Corvette's first complete revision. In addition to the Sting Ray roadster, there now appeared a beautiful grand touring coupe. Each body style sold over 10,000 copies, pushing production to a record 21,000-plus units.

The Sting Ray was strongly influenced by Mitchell's earlier Sting Ray racing car, and his 1959 project XP-720. Design goals for '63 were improved passenger accommodations, more luggage space, better ride and handling, and still higher performance. Mitchell was personally responsible for the '63 coupe's distinctive split window. "If you take that off you might as well forget the whole thing," he said. But Duntov hated it because it reduced visibility, and the feature was dropped in 1964.

Other details of the '63 Sting Ray included hidden headlights, made possible by pivoting sections which were flush with the front end; a dip in the beltline at the trailing edge of the door; coupe doors that cut into the roof; a "gullwing" or dual-cockpit dashboard. The wheelbase was reduced to 98 inches, and frontal area dropped to just one square foot. Yet interior space was increased slightly, and the cockpit was stronger and safer than that of any previous model.

Engines stayed the same in 1963 as they'd been in 1962, but the chassis was improved—expensively—with a three-link independent rear suspension. This unit had double-jointed open drive shafts on either side, control arms, and trailing radius rods. A single transverse leaf spring was mounted to the frame with rubber-cushioned struts. Coils would have been used, but the body lacked sufficient room in this area. Duntov bolted the differential to the rear cross member. The frame was a well-reinforced box. Weight distribution improved to 48/52, from 1962's 53/47. Ride and handling were significantly better, and axle tramp was eliminated. A new recirculating-ball steering gear was combined with dual-arm, three-link balljoint front suspension to make the steering quicker than ever before.

The front brake drums of the '63 were wider than those of the '62 model. The brakes were self-adjusting. An alternator replaced the generator, positive crankcase ventilation was added, and the size of flywheel was reduced. The clutch housing was made of aluminum instead of cast steel. Corvette handling was markedly improved with the new suspension. Road & Track magazine found that the Sting Ray neither hopped up during acceleration nor oversteered on tight bends. Testing a coupe on a series of S-turns, the editors said: "Every time through it, we discovered we could have gone a little faster. We never did find the limit."

General Motors now enjoyed styling that was equal to the Corvette's exciting performance. Some people might quibble over the details of previous models; however, it was hard to fault Mitchell's clean, strong '63 lines and excellent surface development. Intelligently, GM stayed with the basic design for five years. Instead of a restyling every year, the designers merely made detail changes. Most of these were beneficial. Contrary to the Detroit practice of adding trim every year, GM actually removed the stuff. In 1964, for example, slotted wheel discs were added for better brake ventilation, and the fake hood louvers were dropped. The rear quarter vents on the coupe were made partly functional as interior air-exit vents. In 1965 the hood panel was smoothed off and the front fender slots were opened to duct heat out of the engine compartment. The coupe's extractor holes proved inefficient, so in 1966 they were dropped. Also that year, an egg-crate grille appeared. By 1967, the last year for the fourth generation, the Corvette had almost reached perfection. The only '67 styling changes were an oblong backup light, revised front fender louvers, bolt-on instead of knock-off aluminum wheels, and an optional black vinyl covering for the roadster's removable top.

Mechanical evolution was significant in the 1963-67 period. A new fuel-injected, 360-hp small block V8 for 1963 developed 1.15 bhp per cubic inch, and could take a Corvette from 0 to 100 mph in only 15 seconds. For 1965 the Corvette had disc brakes on all four wheels—completely eliminating the fade problem of drum brakes.

The all-time performance V8, the 425-horsepower Mark IV, also appeared in 1965. This engine was

'67 Sting Ray Sport Coupe

1968 Corvette Sport Coupe

adapted for Corvette by Duntov and engineer Jim Premo. The Mark IV displaced 396 cubic inches (bore/stroke 4.09 x 3.76 inches) and replaced the 360-hp small-block option. It had 11.1 compression, four-barrel carburetor and solid valve lifters. Its 425 brake horsepower was accompanied by 416 foot-pounds of torque at 4000 rpm. To handle the power, Duntov equipped the car with stiff front springs, a thick front sway bar, a rear sway bar, a heavy clutch, and a large radiator and fan. Although the Mark IV engine weighed more than 650 pounds, the Corvette's weight distribution remained nearly perfect: 51/49. An aggressive-looking hood bulge and optional side-mounted exhaust pipes completed the impressive package. In 1966, a bore increase to 4.25 inches gave the engine 327 cid.

Acceleration of the big-engine 'Vette was astounding. Timing a 'Vette equipped with a 4.11:1 rear axle ratio, one magazine clocked a 0-60 run of an unbelievable 4.8 seconds, 0-100 in 11.2, and a flat-out maximum of 140 mph. Lower numerical ratios would allow vastly higher top speeds. The only car that could touch it was the 427 Cobra, which was more a competition car than a road car.

In the small-block category, the 327-cid engine was available in six different versions between 1963 and 1967. Carburetored engines offered from 250 to 360 hp; injected models developed 360 to 395. Every form of Corvette was now available—from quiet, civilized tourers to road-gobbling stormers. The public responded enthusiastically. Corvette production was never less than 20,000 in 1963-67: in 1966 it hit 27,720. The convertible outsold the coupe about five to three. Significantly, Corvette's magnificent fourth-generation styling came to an end in 1967, the year just before the advent of federal regulations on crash protection, safety, and exhaust emissions. Taken together, the 1963-67 models represent the most sought-after editions of all Corvette production. They brought the car to its peak as a beautifully engineered, gracefully proportioned, true dual-purpose sports car.

The 1963 Sting Ray was hardly a year old before Mitchell was laying down the shape of its successor. Designs revolved around two separate concepts—a mid-engine Corvette with a sharply raked front end, broad glass area and skirted rear wheels; and a front-engine car based on the experimental Mako Shark II. The Mako derivation won; the high cost of the mid-engine transaxle killed the other idea. David Holls, a car enthusiast and collector, did the production styling. He reveled in his assignment. Holls retained the low front end of the Mako II, but dropped its fastback roofline for a notchback, and developed a Kamm-type rear deck and spoiler. The '68 was well received, despite the fact that it had replaced a classic. This body has continued to sell well right on up to the present, and is now the longest-lived Corvette styling generation.

The '68s used the same engines as the '67s, including the potent L-88. This racing engine produced up to 560 bhp at 6400 rpm, and gulped 103 octane gasoline to satisfy its 12.5:1 compression ratio. It had aluminum heads, oversize valves, aluminum intake manifold, Holley 850 carburetor, and a small-diameter flywheel with a heavy clutch. In 1969 the L88 was joined by the ZL-1 racing engine. It had a dry sump and an aluminum block.

The fifth generation was criticized for excessive glitter and bulkiness, and limited passenger accommodations. GM moved to correct these problems as much as it could in 1969. Its exterior door handles were cleaned up, black-painted grille bars replaced the chrome ones, and the back-up lights blended into inner taillights. Wider rim wheels improved handling, and interior shake was eliminated with a stiffer frame. Room for passengers and luggage was increased. The smaller engine was stroked to 350 cubic inches (bore/stroke 4.00 x 3.48) and offered with 300 or 350 horsepower. Four 427-cid engines were offered, together with an array of axle ratios from 4.56:1 to 2.75:1. The 350 and 427 were the Corvette power plants through 1970. Then in 1971, a 454-cid engine (bore/stroke 4.25 x 4.00) was introduced. It had been designed to meet the tightening federal emissions standards. Meeting the standards left the 350 engine with only 270 gross horsepower in 1972, and the 454 with 365 hp. Both engines had 8.50:1 compression ratios.

AMERICAN SPORTS CARS: CORVETTE

1971 Stingray Coupe

1973 Corvette Coupe

1974 Corvette

1975 Corvette

1978 Corvette

For 1973, all the mechanical-lifter performance engines were dropped. The 350 V8 was rated in net horsepower: 190 to 250. The only Mark IV engine left had 9:1 compression and 275 net horsepower. These alterations did not, however, negatively affect sales. Production was around 38,000 in both '74 and '75; over 46,000 in 1976; close to 50,000 in 1977 and 1978. It had been about 39,000 in 1969; 17,000 in 1970; 22,000 in 1971; and 27,000 in 1972.

Physical changes from 1972 were slight; the addition of a standard burglar alarm was the biggest one. In '73, the windshield wiper cover was dropped, and a five-mph polyurethane "crash bumper" was fitted. Prices accelerated rapidly to over $6,000 by 1975. The Mark IV engine was finally eliminated after 1974, leaving only the 35-cid V8. By 1978, this engine was offering only 185 horsepower at 4000 rpm. Yet the Corvette remained a performance car. One '77 Stingray tested by *Road & Track* beat a Porsche Turbo Carrera through a slalom test and ran from 0 to 60 in 6.8 seconds—half a second quicker than the '73 test model.

Right now, GM ostensibly doesn't know what the Corvette's future will be. For a while it looked like Mitchell's Aerovette, a lovely mid-engine idea car, would be the 1980 model. However, the current Stingray could go on in its present form for several more years, because Chevrolet can still sell more Corvettes than it can build. The Corvette is unique in remaining, as it was in the beginning, America's only production sports car.

The 1979 model offers little change from the past. The "glassback" rear window adopted in 1978 has been retained. The stock differential ratio with automatic is now 3.55:1 instead of 3.08:1. Free-flow mufflers and L82-type air cleaner intakes are used on all engines. But 1979 is just an average year for Corvettes—not vintage like 1957, '63, '65 or '69.

Every Corvette buyer has his prejudices, but the above years represent our picks for today's collector. The 1953-55 vintage is priced out of sight—and not that great a car. Rarity and historical interest are what make it expensive. The '56 is as good a pick as the '57, if you don't mind the milder 265 V8—which may be a blessing in these days of high-priced gasoline. A period of overstyling is represented by the 1958-60 models, and their prices aren't nearly as high as those of the pre-'58s. The 1961-62s are transitional, more handsome cars than their immediate predecessors, but lackluster compared with their immediate successors. Sting Rays of 1963-67 are the most desired models of all, and some command tremendous prices. It's really too early to evaluate the collectibility of post 1967 Corvettes, but the coming of emission, safety, and crash standards has robbed them of the character of earlier cars.

No Corvette is inexpensive anymore. But Corvettes are usually exciting to drive, fun to be seen in, and relatively easy to maintain. And that's why, despite extremely high prices, thousands of people still want to own one.

CROSLEY

Crosley Motors, Inc., Cincinnati, Ohio

If mention of the Crosley makes you chuckle, you just don't have the full picture. True, appliance-builder-turned-auto-mogul Powel Crosley, Jr., built a lot of funny little cars between 1939 and 1952—underpowered tin crates that would have been better used as bumper cars than genuine automobiles. But he also built the Hot Shot and the Super Sports. Those two models were sports cars as genuine as the Jaguar XK-120.

The Super Sports came with a set of doors; the Hot Shot had none. Neither car came off the showroom floor in raceable condition. Typical performance was: 0-60 in 20 seconds; top speed 77 mph; standing-start quarter-mile in 25 seconds at 66 mph. What gave the Crosleys race potential was the speed equipment offered by accessory houses. Companies such as Vertex, Newhouse, S.CO.T., Braje, H&C, and J.C. Whitney could turn the cute little roadsters into near-100-mph rockets, and cut their 0-60 time almost in half—and cheaply. For instance, Braje offered a full-race cam for $25, headers for $28, dual carburetor manifolds (using twin Amal motorcycle carbs) for $60, and finned aluminum cam covers for $15. High-performance ignition was sold by H&C and Vertex; S.CO.T. built a Roots-type supercharger which increased Crosley horsepower from the standard 26.5 to 55 bhp.

Since the Crosley engine weighed about 150 pounds, two men could wrestle it out of the car and work it over on a table. Or you could buy a bare chassis for about $800 and wrap a streamlined racing body around the souped-up mill. That's not to say the stock sports bodies were heavy—a '52 S.S. weighed only 1,250 pounds.

Despite legends about what speed equipment does to buzzy little engines, the Crosley four held up well under performance treatment. In 1949 Crosley dropped its unsuccessful sheet-metal engine for a conventional cast-iron block. Using five main bearings and full-pressure lubrication, the 44-cid 1949-52 engine was strong, and could be revved to 10,000 rpm.

Late 1949 and all 1950 sports cars also had outstanding front brakes—outstanding when they worked. They were spot discs made by Goodyear-Hawley, derived from aircraft, and were impervious to fade. But they lacked good sealing, so they often froze solid when exposed to salt or road grime. In 1951-52 Crosley used Bendix drums. Even these more conventional binders were capable of hauling a Crosley down from high speeds without difficulty.

The cars' handling was something nobody needed to modify. The Hot Shot/SS 85-inch wheelbase spanned a strong steel frame. There was an I-beam axle with semi-elliptic leaf springs and tube shocks up front; a solid axle, tube shocks and quarter elliptics in back. Primitive as this system seems, the cars stuck to the road like magnets.

If such specifications suggested that the two-seaters were capable sports cars, their competition record proved it. In 1950 a Crosley won the Index of Performance in the Sebring 12 Hours. In 1951 Briggs Cunningham entered another Crosley in Le Mans; it too was a cinch for the Index until a bad voltage regulator forced it into retirement.

The Hot Shot appeared in 1949, priced at only $849. It lasted through 1952, at which time it sold for $952. The Super Sports was a 1950 introduction at $925; by the end of production in 1952, its price had risen to $1,029. The prices were astonishingly low, considering the fun and performance the little cars provided—especially if the owner was willing to spend a little time and money in modifications. But perhaps they were priced too low to make any money for the company.

Whether the problem was low price or low production, Powel Crosley gave up the auto business after 1952. Production had peaked in 1948, when he'd sold nearly 25,000 cars. By 1950 it had dropped to 7,000, and in 1952 it barely reached 1,500. Sports-car production was 725 in 1949 (all Hot Shots); 742 in 1950; 646 in 1951; and 358 in 1952. Altogether, 2,498 two-seaters were built. Perhaps 100 of them are still around. Despite their good performance, they don't command high prices today. You can buy a fine one for $2,000, and a "runner" for $750. Crosleys are one of the happy exceptions to the collector's rule that anything worthwhile costs big money.

1952 Crosley Super Sports

CUNNINGHAM

B. S. Cunningham Co., West Palm Beach, Florida

From 1950 through 1955, Briggs Swift Cunningham paved the way for America's successful onslaught on international racing in the 1960s. The Ford GTs of a decade later would be backed by a multibillion-dollar corporation; Cunningham had only his private fortune with which to finance his car. That Cunningham came close to winning Le Mans on several occasions is a tremendous credit to his tenacity.

Sports-racing cars like the Cunningham C-2R, and C-4R through C-6R, are not the focus of this book, though they are inextricably bound to the C-1 and C-3 road machines. It is impossible to mention the C-1 and C-3 without mentioning the others.

Cunningham, a wealthy Cincinnatian, was good at every sport he tried: yachting, shooting, flying, golfing—and driving. After World War II, Cunningham joined the infant Sports Car Club of America. He finished second at Watkins Glen in 1948 with his amazingly successful hybrid, the "Bumerc"—a Buick engine and chassis combined with a Mercedes-Benz SSK-type body.

At the Glen, Cunningham met Phil Walters and Bill Frick, who interested him in their "Fordillac"—a Ford body and chassis with a Cadillac V8 engine. Briggs bought the Walters-Frick company. His goal was to build a sports car for the Le Mans 24 Hours, the world's premier endurance race.

Unfortunately, the Fordillac didn't qualify for Le Mans because it was not a "real" car. It was a hot rod, an amalgam of two different makes. Cunningham loved the new lightweight Cadillac overhead-valve V8, so he decided instead to enter all-Cadillac machines in the 1950 endurance classic.

A Cadillac at Le Mans? Yes, and the result was impressive. Cunningham entered two cars: a stock Coupe de Ville, and an aerodynamic racer nicknamed "Le Monstre" by the French for its size and aggressive appearance. Le Monstre hit 134 mph on the Mulsanne Straight; the Coupe de Ville hit 115. They finished an amazing 10th and 11th overall. The stock car finished first: Cunningham had dumped "Le Monstre" into a sandbank and lost a half an hour digging it out. He'd also driven the last few hours in high gear, Le Monstre having lost both first and second gears.

Cunningham as well as the French authorities were convinced that Cadillacs were too big and unwieldy for Le Mans, a twisty course. So Briggs spent late 1950 preparing his own sports car—the first Cunningham. Designated C-1, this car was powered by the Chrysler FirePower 331-cid hemi-head V8. Cunningham pre-

ferred the hemi to the Cadillac V8, although he did use the GM division lighter Cadillac pistons, which raised the hemi's compression from 7.5:1 to 8.3:1 and increased horsepower by 10 percent. The C-1's horsepower was somewhere around 220.

The car had been designed chiefly by body engineer Bob Blake, assisted by Bud Unger, although everyone from the boss on down had had a hand in the project. Cunningham viewed the design goal as "a matter of what we liked" but *Mechanix Illustrated's* Tom McCahill called it "a polyglot selection of the world's finest." He said, "From any angle you can find the best of several other great cars." The grille, for example, looked like that of the Ferrari Barchetta, or one of the later Chrysler-Ghia sports cars. The overall lines were clean and purposeful.

The C-1 used an extremely strong tubular steel chassis with coil-spring independent front suspension and a De Dion rear axle. Its wheelbase was 105 inches, its width was 70 inches, and its track was 58 inches. The cockpit contained a full set of instruments including an oil temperature gauge and a pair of $300 leather bucket seats. The C-1 was lavishly trimmed compared with European counterparts, but Briggs Cunningham's attitude toward its luxury was casual: "They were more road cars in a way, because we used to drive them everywhere. . . .That was what we wanted them to do—drive to the race, then run on the track." Cunningham was asking nothing more of his automobiles than sports-car builders had asked for decades. The one-off C-1 is now on display with other Cunninghams at the Cunningham museum in Costa Mesa, California.

The C-1 accurately prefigured the shape of the following C-2R. Ostensibly, the C-2 was available in road trim, but only three were built, and all carried the "R" (racing) designation. The C-2 used the C-1's 105-inch wheelbase and sophisticated suspension. Its worm-and-roller steering was quick—only 2¾ turns lock-to-lock. The brakes were drums. They used Raybestos linings and were carefully ventilated. Again Chrysler supplied the engine. The C-2R was a tremendously powerful car. In "street tune" it could hit 100 mph in second gear, and 124 in high. One C-2R was timed at 152 mph. Cunningham had great hopes for it in the 1951 Le Mans race. And for a while, it didn't disappoint him.

Early in the race, which started in a downpour, two C-2Rs spun out and were eliminated. But the third, driven by Walters and John Fitch, took off like a bullet and ran strongly through the night. By dawn, it was in

1952 C-4RK

The C-4RK, with 220 horsepower

second place, behind a C-type racing Jaguar. But this didn't last. The C-2R was heavy, about 4,000 pounds fully laden, and its high compression caused detonation on low-octane French gasoline. The "ping" eventually began to endanger the bearings, and Walters and Fitch had to back off. They finished 18th.

The racers went back to the drawing board for Le Mans 1952, and Cunningham built the first of his models that could be bought in a showroom: the C-3. Its price was around $10,000. The car had a lovely four-place coupe body designed by Giovanni Michelotti of Vignale, the Turin coachworks. A cabriolet model was added later. Vignale's construction technique may have been of the body-putty variety typical of Italian houses of that period. But, also typically Italian, the car's styling was magnificent. Arthur Drexler, curator of New York's Museum of Modern Art, named the coupe to his list of the world's 10 best cars. It shared this distinction with such tours de force as the Cisitalia coupe by Pininfarina. Together with Bob Bourke's marvelous 1953 Studebaker Starliner hardtop, the C-3 represented America on a list that was otherwise completely European.

A total of 27 C-3's, 18 coupes and nine roadsters, were built. Their main purpose had been to qualify the Cunningham as a "production" car, so that it could qualify for production-class racing. But they were great buys for the money, and for three years sold as fast as Cunningham could turn them out.

For Le Mans 1952 Cunningham entered his most successful racing car yet, the C-4R. With 325 Chrysler horses, a low, aggressive snout and a 100-inch wheelbase, the C-4R demonstrated that Cunningham had learned well from his 1951 Le Mans experience. The C-4R weighed only 3,000 pounds. Its drum brakes were finned and ventilated.

Two roadsters and a kammback coupe, the C-4RK, were built. With Chrysler's help, the engines were redesigned to accept low-octane gasoline. Driving one of the coupes himself for 20 of LeMans's 24 hours, Cunningham finished fourth, behind two Mercedes-Benzes and a Nash-Healey. In the five-to-eight-liter

class, he broke the distance record established in 1950 by a Cadillac-powered Allard.

The year had been gratifying, but Cunningham still hungered for victory at LeMans. In 1953 he was back again, with two C-4Rs and the new, hairier C-5R. The C-5R had been designed by Cunningham. It was a long, low coupe—sleeker than the C-4RK. In addition to the usual Chrysler engine, it had torsion-bar suspension, a straight front axle, Hallibrand knock-off wheels, and 11-inch AL-Fin brakes. Cunningham had

The C-5R, long, low, and hairy

The C-5R, third place at Le Mans, 1953

worked on the valving problem, which had beset two of his C-4Rs the year before. It looked like an unstoppable car.

Fitch and Walters drove the C-5R, following a carefully planned lap average which had been calculated to put them in the winner's circle at the end of 24 hours. The C-5R performed flawlessly, hitting 156 mph down the long Mulsanne Straight. But the Jaguar D-types were quicker. The C-5R finished third, surrounded by Jaguars, which took first, second and fourth. The two C-4Rs came in seventh and 10th.

Jaguar's big advantage that year was not in performance, but in brakes. Briggs had ordered Dunlop-Girling disc brakes for all his Le Mans cars, but the British company didn't deliver. Cunningham had been told just before the race that the discs would not be available until later in the year. Some observers have said they suspect Dunlop was acting in Jaguar's interests, but nobody is sure.

The Cunningham team came to Le Mans '54 with three cars: two old C-4Rs and a 4.5-liter Ferrari. Its latest design, the C-6R, wasn't ready in time. The Ferrari retired with rear axle troubles. The two-year-old C-4Rs again performed well, finishing third and fifth.

The 1955 Le Mans entry was the C-6R, the last of the Cunninghams. Fitted with a 2942 Offenhauser Indianapolis-type engine to keep it under the new three-liter displacement limit, it lacked the durability of the Chrysler-powered cars, and failed to finish. This race was overshadowed by the frightening accident of Pierre Levegh, whose Mercedes-Benz broke loose and killed 80 spectators. Walters came in shaken and told Cunningham he didn't feel like driving anymore. Many of his fellows felt likewise. It took a lot of time for most of them to climb back into racing cockpits after the most tragic accident in Le Mans history.

Although the C-6R was later tried unsuccessfully with a Jaguar engine, Cunningham wound up his company in 1955. It wasn't a result of the Levegh crash, or (as is so often reported) that the street cars were losing money. Cunningham says: "We just broke even on the production cars," but that didn't mean the whole factory did. The race cars were money completely down the drain. Still they gave us publicity for the production cars, and what we'd have done without it I don't know. But in those days if you lost $50,000 or more for five consecutive seasons you were classified as a 'hobby' by the tax people—and you can't deduct money spent for a hobby.

"The cars, basically, were just too big and too heavy. Everybody else was getting lighter and smaller. We didn't have an engine—the Corvette wasn't built yet. We didn't have a gearbox—we had to have that built in Germany. We were just getting outclassed. . . .Meyer-Drake was asking $100,000 apiece for redesigned engines. The cost is all in the tool work, and if the engine isn't successful you have to develop it, get the bugs out. There just isn't time."

Briggs Cunningham continued to race other people's cars—Jaguars, Oscas, Formula Juniors, and Corvettes—until 1963. Then he retired from the circuits to spend his time on his museum. But he had written a great story at Le Mans. Nobody else has come anywhere near such success on a shoestring budget.

The only Cunningham that collectors can still buy is, of course, the C-3. Most of the 27 C-3s built are still around. But pedigree costs money, and rarity adds to the price. The Cunningham buyer will not be disappointed with his purchase, but it will be expensive.

1951 Cunningham C-1

Cunningham C-1

Interior view of the Cunningham C-1

DEVIN

Devin Motors, Los Angeles, California

The Devin story starts in 1952. Bill Devin was a sports-car dealer in Los Angeles, where he and his partner, Ernie McAfee, sold exotic cars like Siatas and Ferraris to wealthy racers like Phil Hill and Masten Gregory. Devin received a particularly pretty Ermini 1100 which he sold to racer Jim Orr. But before he sold the car, he made a fiberglass mold of the Ermini's aluminum Scaglietti body.

Devin then invented a system of modular molds that would enable him to alter the dimensions of the Scaglietti design to fit a wide variety of cars. The Devin body kit could be ordered to fit wheelbases of 78 to 106 inches, and tread widths of 40 to 52 inches. Devin's modular system was much more efficient than those of competitors: other makers of fiberglass body kits used a separate mold for each body size. He was then able to sell a complete sports-car body for just $295. It came with a sleek headrest for racing, or with a complete interior, folding top, and windshield for street use.

Thousands of sports cars received fiberglass Devin bodies in the middle-to-late 1950s. For only a few hundred dollars, an enthusiast could transform his humdrum TR-3, MGA, Austin-Healey or Corvette into a beautiful Italian-style roadster—one that would look almost identical with a Ferrari Mondial that cost 20 times as much. Devin sold body kits as fast as his crew

could pop them out of the molds. He soon began thinking about selling completed cars himself.

At the very moment Devin was deciding to build and sell his own high-performance sports car, he received an intriguing order from an Irish engineer named Malcolm MacGregor. MacGregor wanted a Devin body kit to fit a chassis he was building to accept a Corvette V8 engine. It was a heaven-sent opportunity for Devin. After a few months of transmission planning, Devin and MacGregor formed Devonshire Engineering, with the goal of building sports-car chassis in Belfast.

MacGregor's chassis was state-of-the-art in 1957— more advanced than anything being built in the United States, and the equal of any limited-production sports-racing car from Europe. MacGregor started with steel tubing, three inches in diameter. He constructed a ladder-type frame with tubular loops at the cowl and behind the seats, which not only supplemented the sturdy tubular crossmembers, but acted as rollbars in case of an accident. This frame was very similar to that used by AC Cars for the Ace, which later became the Cobra 289.

MacGregor fitted this frame with a fully independent rear suspension, including De Dion tube; coil springs; dual parallel trailing arms; and huge, 11-inch Girling disc brakes mounted inboard next to the differential. At

1962 Devin SS

AMERICAN SPORTS CARS: DEVIN

the front he used parallel A-arms with coil springs and tubular shock absorbers, along with another pair of Girling discs. MacGregor's chassis, then, was one of the first to offer all-independent suspension and four-wheel disc brakes on a production car. Dunlop wire wheels and tires finished off MacGregor's contribution.

This rolling chassis was shipped to El Monte, California, where Devin and his crew completed the car. A stock Corvette 283-cid V8, fitted with a special low-profile manifold and carburetor to fit under the Devin's low hood, was bolted in along with the Borg-Warner T-10 four-speed transmission used in Corvettes.

Devin designed a new, even better-looking version of his stock kit body, this one with a larger grille opening that would increase air flow to the canted Corvette radiator. This beautiful fiberglass shell—half an inch thick in some places—was bonded to the chassis and was trimmed out with high-quality Stewart-Warner instruments, leather bucket seats, and a wood-rimmed steering wheel. Street versions had a folding top and side-curtains, which were similar to those used by many British sports cars.

Devin called his new car the Devin SS. It was remarkable. The SS could run 0-60 mph in 4.8 seconds, and 0-100 in 12 seconds. Its top speed was over 140 mph. This made it just about the fastest street machine available in 1957—almost five seconds faster to 100 mph than a fuel-injected Corvette of the same vintage. And the price for this incredible performance was just $5,950—less than a comparably equipped Corvette or Jaguar, and half the price of Ferrari and Maserati models that offered comparable performance.

Determined to prove his car in competition, Devin sponsored Californian Peter Woods in SCCA class C-modified racing. Woods won the C-modified national championship in 1959, beating all sorts of fancier, more expensive, but slower sports-racing models. The Devin SS was obviously one of the best cars of its type in the world.

Yet the cars didn't sell. The Devin SS was in production from early 1958 through the end of 1961, during which time exactly 15 were sold. In 1960, Devin raised the car's price to $10,000, since it was obvious that he would not be able to sell many cars at any price. He was right. People were no more eager to buy an SS at $10,000 than they were at $5,950.

When Devin realized that the car would not take off by itself, he contacted Chevrolet, and tried to talk the GM division into bankrolling a limited-production run of 100. That would have at least moved the Devin SS from the C-modified to the C-production class. His efforts were fruitless: Chevrolet was still observing a corporate ban on racing participation. In the end, there were simply no buyers for the Devin SS, and the whole project collapsed after just a handful of cars had been built.

Devin had other irons in the fire. In 1959 he restyled his original body kit again, giving it a high trunk into which a Volkswagen engine fit like a hand in a glove. He built a frame of square tubing and bonded it to a fiberglass undertray. This was planned to take stock Volkswagen suspension components. The interior was fitted with bucket seats. The car, which Devin called the Devin D, was available as a kit for only $1,495, or as a complete car for just $2,950. It was a pretty, reliable, and surprisingly sophisticated sports car. Hundreds of Devin Ds were sold, as well as Devin Cs—the same chassis equipped with a Chevy Corvair power plant.

Unfortunately for Devin, by the mid-1960s that smooth, Scaglietti-styled body for which his cars were famous had come to look old-fashioned. His body kits had been fairly profitable in their day, but the Devin SS and Devin C and D were too costly to produce for their limited market. Eventually, Devin got out of the car business completely and founded a company to manufacture bumpers and ladders for motor homes.

The Devin SS was the high point of Devin's career. The car may not have been very successful from a conventional point of view—only 15 units produced and one national championship won in four years—yet it's still an important milestone in the development of the American sports car.

1964 Devin

AMERICAN SPORTS CAR SHOWCASE 1

A parade of nimble, gutsy machines
that have won many laurels
and a place in the hearts
of car buffs everywhere.

1920 Mercer raceabout

1923 Stutz Bearcat

1929 Stutz Blackhawk

1970 AMX II

1970 AMX III

1957 Corvette

1959 Corvette

1963 Corvette

1977 Corvette

1951 Cunningham C-1

1952 Cunningham E4RK

1953 Cunningham C-5R

1951 Excalibur J

Prototype 1955 **Ford Thunderbird**

1957 Ford Thunderbird

DUAL-GHIA

Dual Motors Corp., Detroit, Michigan

Most exotic cars are the products of a single imaginative individual. The Dual-Ghia is no exception. In this case the individual was Eugene Casaroll, owner of Automobile Shippers, Inc., a Detroit trucking firm. Casaroll's company made most of its money moving new Chrysler cars from the factory to dealers and distributors. The boss favored Chrysler's automobiles. A car enthusiast who sponsored his own entries in the Indianapolis 500, Casaroll also dreamed about a luxury sports car he would build if he could.

In 1952 Virgil Exner, Chrysler stylist, teamed up with the Ghia coachworks in Italy to produce the Dodge Firearrow. One part of a long parade of Ghia-built prototypes conceived by Exner, the Firearrow was Exner's attempt to put an end to Dodge's dowdy image. It was a typical show car, conjured up to excite the public with the promise of fabulous new models.

The Firearrow impressed Casaroll. When William Newberg, Dodge Division president, announced that the car would not be produced by his company, Casaroll approached Newberg for the design rights. The concept seemed perfect for a limited edition. This sleek, luxurious Italian-styled body was mounted on an ordinary American chassis which had mechanical components any gas station could service. Casaroll recruited designer Paul Farrago to work with Ghia in producing a running prototype.

Farrago and Ghia built two initial prototypes, called Firebombs. Working to redesign the Firearrow's impractical mid-grille bumper and tiny trunk, Farrago gradually refined and improved the package. The prototypes provided increased legroom front and back: they were true four-passenger sports cars. They had far more trunk space than the Dodge original; a conventional, heavy front bumper; and dual instead of quad headlights. The Firebomb was scheduled for release in late 1955, priced at $5,500—an astoundingly low price. The production car did not emerge until mid-1956. By then its name had been changed to Dual-Ghia, and it had adopted the faddish wraparound windshield of '56 Chrysler production models. Its price was $7,650.

Dual-Ghias were available with two engines. Standard was the 230 horsepower, 315-cid Dodge Red Ram V8. Optional at $100 extra was a "Super Firebomb," a 260-hp engine with Dodge D-500 specification: 9.25:1 compression ratio, hemispherical head combustion chamber, solid valve lifters, special cam,

The Firearrow, an attempt to alter Dodge's dowdy image

AMERICAN SPORTS CARS: DUAL-GHIA

and Mallory ignition. A "Stage 2" Firebomb engine could also be ordered. Its dual four-barrel carburetors raised horsepower to 285.

Powerflite automatic transmission with a floor shift lever was standard equipment on all Dual-Ghias. It was coupled to a "performance" rear axle ratio of 3.54:1. Power steering and power brakes were optional. The suspension was set up for stable handling instead of a cushy ride. Oriflow shock absorbers were used, along with the biggest brakes Casaroll could buy from Chrysler. The chassis, modified from a stock Dodge unit by Giovanni Savonuzzi, Ghia's chief engineer, measured 115 inches in wheelbase and had a "step-down" floor like that of the Hudson Hornet. Since the engine was set fairly far to the rear, the car's weight distribution was almost 50-50.

To hold costs down, Casaroll decided to assemble his Dual-Ghia partly in Italy and partly in the States. The stock Dodge chassis was sent to Turin, where it was modified and the smooth sports-car body was fitted to it. In Detroit, Dual Motors installed the engine, transmission, and interior trim. Although some duty had to be paid on the imported parts, the overall cost of assembly in this way was much lower than it would have been had all production work been done in America. Estimates of the Dual-Ghia's cost if fully assembled in the U.S. ran as high as $15,000 then—about $40,000 in today's money.

The Italians' reputation for excessive use of body putty notwithstanding, the Dual-Ghia's body was beautifully built. It was made in the traditional Torino fashion: a craftsman with a pair of snips literally cut out each piece of metal, then hammered it into shape over an aluminum die. The panels were put together with efficient welding and a minimum of filler. Bright metal trim pieces—like wheel covers, grille, windshield frame, and door handles—were made of brass, then chrome-plated three times. The side-trim clip holders also were made of brass.

Upholstery in the Dual-Ghia was well up to the car's exterior trim standards. Every wear surface was upholstered. The trunk, for example, was lined with black felt, under the hood was quilted leather, sandwiching fiberglass insulation. Dual Motors used top-quality Connolly English leather for the seats. Those seats were built with coil springs, and were padded with foam rubber—like living-room furniture. The dashboard knobs and instruments came from Chrysler parts bins, but they were laid out in a practical and unified fashion. A big speedometer and tachometer flanked a central clock just under the steering wheel; below the big instruments were the usual small gauges for oil pressure, fuel level, amperes, and water temperature. Control buttons and radio knobs lined the center of the dash to the right of the instruments.

Though the Dual-Ghia weighed more than 3,599 pounds, it was fast. *Motor Trend* magazine, testing a 260-hp version in August 1956, clocked four successive 0-60 sprints in an average 8.2 seconds. "The next check, 50-80, made me even more of a convert," wrote Don MacDonald, "for I averaged a fantastic 7.9 seconds. Top speed between mile posts on a still afternoon was 124 mph!"

MacDonald had two complaints about the Dual-Ghia: the steering was restricted by a limited front fender clearance, and the Italian-designed window winders required an incredible 11 turns to move the windows from one stop to the other. Casaroll must have read *Motor Trend.* Almost immediately he corrected the wheel clearance problem; shortly after production began, he replaced the window cranks with electric motors.

The $10,000 Mark II Continental of 1956-57 received much publicity as a result of the claim that one's social standing determined one's eligibility to buy the car. This was partly just hot air. However, Casaroll planned

1958 Dual-Ghia

DeSoto Adventurer II (left) and two Dodge Firearrows

to build only 150 Dual-Ghias a year, and personally went over every purchase order with a copy of the Social Register in hand. Frank Sinatra and Peter Lawford were allowed two of the first Dual-Ghias off the line; Dean Martin and Sammy Davis, Jr., were turned down. (Martin finally did buy one in the 1960s.) Other Hollywood luminaries awarded Dual-Ghia ownership included Lucille Ball, Eddie Fisher, Hoagy Carmichael, David Rose, and swimsuit magnate Fred Cole. One rich New York socialite was turned down because New York's allotment of cars was spoken for. She offered to move to Connecticut; but Connecticut's allotment was gone too. Wrote columnist Dorothy Kilgallen: "The Rolls-Royce is the status symbol for those who can't get a Dual-Ghia."

Unfortunately, like many other dreamers, Casaroll was unable to produce more than a fraction of his planned output. Between 1956 and 1958, his factory turned out only 117 cars—102 convertibles, two special hardtops, and 13 various prototypes. His problem wasn't a lack of orders; the real hang-up was the time it took to put a Dual-Ghia together. According to Bruce Wennerstrom, Dual-Ghia historian, "Some 1,300 man-hours were lavished by Ghia on each body . . . .Dual Motors spent another 200 hours on final assembly." Casaroll himself said "the Dual-Ghia is intended for the car lover and, I am proud to say, is built by men who can claim that title by right of their art."

Casaroll also was not charging enough to cover his costs. He was losing at least $4,000 on each Dual-Ghia sold. By the time he ran out of his initial supply of engines and chassis, Chrysler had switched to unit body-chassis construction. This made Chrysler's old separate chassis unavailable. Dual Motors was faced with the choice of building a new model or giving up.

You can't say Casaroll didn't try. His first move was to investigate Exner's fantastic Dart show car—a long, Chrysler-based four-seater with a retractable hardtop. Casaroll built one prototype, which had an ungainly concave grille and fins almost as big as the Dart's. He didn't like the prototype, and gave it up. He then asked Ghia to design a new car from the ground up.

The result, which appeared in August 1960, was the beautiful L6.4, the prettiest Dual-Ghia ever built.

Forsaking the tailfins of previous models, the L6.4 was an exciting shape. Its lines were faintly reminiscent of Exner's 1961 Plymouth. It had a smooth deck, semi-outrigger taillights, and a neat crease along the body sides. The grille, defined by a strong hood bulge, retained a resemblance to previous models with its rounded oblong shape and single horizontal bar. The roofline was a semi-fastback; the glass began just behind the C pillar and tapered cleanly into the deck.

Lacking a stock chassis to work with, Ghia was forced to design the L6.4's chassis from scratch. Its wheelbase was 115 inches, as before; but its length grew by seven inches to 210. And the new car was slightly wider than previous models. Unlike the first generation D-6s, which used body parts from every Chrysler division, the L6.4 was made up of few stock Chrysler components. A Chrysler convertible windshield was the most obvious. Custom-built bumpers, wheel covers, body panels and standard air conditioning added to the L6.4's cost. Ultimately, the L6.4 listed at $13,000 in Italy, or $15,000 f.o.b. Detroit.

By 1960 Chrysler had abandoned the hemi-head V8, so Casaroll switched to the 383-cid wedge-head engine, which developed 325 horsepower. No performance options were available. The chassis was more softly sprung than those of previous Dual automobiles. Nevertheless, the L6.4 was adequate on the road. It would still reach 60 mph from rest in less than 10 seconds, and could approach 120 mph.

Only 26 of the L6.4s were built between 1961 and 1963. After that, Dual Motors folded. Casaroll died in the late '60s. His planned third-generation Dual-Ghia never saw production. The majority of the surviving D-Gs are 1956-58 models; most were sold in the U.S.

There was a time, not too long ago, when collectors could pick up Dual-Ghias in good condition for $5,000 or so. That time is gone forever. Today, it takes about $15,000—the original list price of the L6.4 some 20 years ago—to buy any Dual-Ghia. The car's advantages are its made-in-U.S.A. mechanical components, its interesting looks, its exclusivity, and the fact that most models still around are in good shape. As an investment, it's not hot. Prices will take awhile to climb above their present levels.

EDWARDS

Edwards Engineering Co., South San Francisco, California

While wealthy industrialist Eugene Casaroll was dreaming in Detroit, wealthy industrialist Sterling H. Edwards was dreaming in San Francisco. Both men had the same vision: an exclusive, low-production, luxury sports car. Casaroll had considerable clout with Chrysler, ample space for production, and some stylist friends in Italy; Edwards could rely on only home-grown stylists, a very small factory, and whatever engine and chassis parts he could lay his hands on. Casaroll built 143 Dual-Ghias; Edwards made only six of his Americas.

The first Edwards Special appeared in 1949. It was a four-seat convertible with removable hardtop and windshield. The idea was that these civilities could be quickly removed for racing. Edwards did race, and enjoyed some success in SCCA competition.

The Special weighed only 2,500 pounds, or 2,000 pounds when stripped for racing. The chassis was a sophisticated chrome-molybdenum tubular unit, equipped with independent suspension all around, disc brakes, and a hot Ford V8 engine. To stay within the 1500cc displacement limit, the Ford engine was cut to 122 cubic inches. Making up for the loss in displacement were dual Stromberg carburetors, 11:1 compression, overhead valves, and a hot cam. The prototype developed 115 horsepower at 5300 rpm, and could do about 115 mph flat out.

Edward's second experimental was built in 1951, with several cost-saving components. It used a 100-inch-wheelbase Henry J chassis, and a carefully assembled fiberglass body. This car had power—it used a 331-cid Chrysler hemi V8. But it oversteered with abandon and suffered from chassis flex. Edwards went back to the drawing board.

The "production" Edwards America was announced in late 1953. It was a slab-sided, good-looking four-seat convertible, with a large rectangular egg-crate grille and 1952 Mercury taillights. The instrument panel and steering wheel were Oldsmobile parts. The interior was upholstered in leather. The first America retained the Henry J chassis, but used a 303.7-cid Oldsmobile V8 instead of the hemi. It had a target price of $4,995.

The other five Edwards Americas used different engines. Two of them had 205-hp Lincoln V8s; three had 210-hp Cadillacs. Greater rigidity was provided by the Mercury station wagon chassis, sectioned to a wheelbase of 107 inches.

By 1955 an Edwards cost over $7,800. All models came standard with electric window lifts, Hydra-Matic transmission, and Kelsey-Hayes wire wheels. Their high price kept demand extremely low. Even if there had been plenty of buyers, it's questionable that Edwards's small workshop and time-consuming hand construction methods could have turned out enough Americas to meet demand.

After developing a pretty hardtop model in early 1955, Edwards gave up on his project. Today he manufactures steel cable and wire in San Francisco.

The aggressive-looking Edwards America

EXCALIBUR

Brooks Stevens/SS Cars/Excalibur Motors, Milwaukee, Wisconsin

Among the thousands of people who, by various stretches of the imagination, lay claim to the title "car stylist," Brooks Stevens is unique. He has raced, rallied, collected and built cars, as well as styled them. And he still builds them today. His Excalibur roadsters and phaetons of 1979 invoke the spirit, if not the exact style, of the classic Mercedes-Benz SSK. Stevens is unique in at least one other respect. He is the only man ever to build a competitive sports car out of a Henry J chassis and a Willys engine.

The Excalibur J appeared in 1952. Stevens was then a design consultant to Kaiser-Frazer Corp., and had a direct pipeline to Henry J. Kaiser. As a racing driver, Stevens had asked himself: Why not build an inexpensive, dual-purpose sports car on the Henry J chassis? Kaiser encouraged him. The K-F's fortuitous acquisition of Willys-Overland made it possible for Stevens to use the overhead-valve F-head Willys six. This was a much better engine than the Henry J's, though the two mills had come from the same design roots.

Stevens built three Excalibur Js on the 100-inch-wheelbase Henry J chassis. The chassis were strengthened, and were fitted with metallic brake linings and knock-off wire wheels. The F-head Willys engine displaced 161 cubic inches (bore/stroke 3.125x3.5 inches), and originally produced 90 horsepower. Stevens modified it with exhaust headers, static and dynamic balancing, three carburetors, and hot ignition. By the time he was through, horsepower was up around 125. Stevens says: "Barney Roos, Willys' consulting engineer, told me that if I turned the engine over 5500 rpm, it would go through the hood. We turned it consistently at 6500 . . . ."

The Excalibur J body design was primitive—of the Lotus Seven school rather than the Corvette school. A low, squat radiator blended into a squared-off hood. The front fenders were freestanding. Exhausts sprouted out the sides. The car was a two-seater having rudimentary trunk space and simple weather protection. Stevens believed it could be built to sell for "definitely below $3,000 and preferably nearer to $2,000. The weight factor will be low and the performance should be exciting."

He was right about performance. He raced the cars for two years, hoping to convince Kaiser to put the Excalibur into production. In 24 races, Excalibur Js took nine firsts, seven seconds and four thirds in Class D-Modified. Their most important win was at the 1953 U. S. Grand Prix. There Hal Ullrich took first in class and third overall. *Road & Track* magazine reported:

Brooks Stevens driving the 1952 Excalibur J

AMERICAN SPORTS CARS: EXCALIBUR

Excalibur J at speed

Stevens rendering of hardtop Excalibur J

Excalibur racing car

Rendering of racer by Stevens

"He gave the customers quite a show with his superb cornering and power on the straightaway. . .cornering and accelerating right along with the big ones." Often in its racing career, the bug-like Excalibur trounced such expensive and potent competition as the 2.7-liter Ferrari, Jaguar XK-120 MC, Cunningham, and Allard.

Kaiser-Frazer chose the more civilized (and anything but race-bred) Kaiser-Darrin for its sports-car project, and later went out of business. Stevens continued to race his Excaliburs until 1958, when his supply of engines dried up. "We rebuilt one car with a GMC-blown Jaguar C-type engine, with which Hal Ullrich and Carl Haas won Class B-Modified at the Elkhart 500, to take the national championship," Stevens says."The decline of Kaiser-Frazer, of course, made the whole project untenable, though road versions of the Excalibur J with three-speed overdrive transmission, windshield, top and side curtains were available on special order. . . ." These versions could achieve 100 mph. The three racing Excalibur Js are displayed at Brooks Stevens' museum in Mequon, Wisconsin.

The next model was a sports-racing car, the Excalibur Hawk. It was built around a Studebaker Hawk suspension and 289-cid supercharged V8. Its aluminum body, with prominent fins, and low, sweeping nose, was wrapped around a tubular space frame. The Excalibur Hawk was unsuccessful, however. The day of big-inch front-engine racing cars was over, and the Hawk was retired after 1963.

Finally, Stevens came up with his best-known Excalibur, a replica-like roadster based on the Mercedes-Benz SSK. Built on a modified Studebaker Lark chassis, the Excalibur made its debut at the New York Automobile Show in 1963. Studebaker had originally sponsored the project, but fearing the car would compete with the Hawk and Avanti, the company ordered Stevens not to display it. Infuriated, Stevens rented his own space at the show, and exhibited the car as the "Studebaker SS." Subsequently, he founded SS Automobiles, and began limited production.

The Excalibur SS was an exciting car. It was a progenitor of today's replicas, but built with far greater integrity than most of them. The engine was originally a Studebaker supercharged 289 V8 which produced one horsepower per cubic inch. It was positioned far back in the chassis, for perfect 50-50 weight distribution. *Road & Track* magazine, testing the car in 1964, recorded a 0-60 acceleration time of 7 seconds, and a shattering standing-start quarter mile time of 15 seconds at 92 mph. The original body was aluminum, but Stevens soon switched to fiberglass, and fiberglass is still being used today.

Studebaker having gone out of business by 1966, Stevens looked around for another engine. His canny selection was the light, powerful 327-cid Corvette V8 with Corvette drive train, provided by his friends Ed Cole and S. E. Knudsen of General Motors. By this time Excalibur production had exceeded 120 cars. Stevens had become America's sixth largest automobile manufacturer—after the four major companies and Checker.

Excalibur Hawk

Excalibur Series III roadster

Exactly when the Excalibur stopped being a sports car is debatable. But a clear transformation occurred in 1965, when the cycle-fendered original was joined by a heavier open car which had full fenders and running boards. Later a 2+2 phaeton was added to the line, and the light roadster was phased out.

These first Excaliburs were produced until 1970, when Stevens introduced the Series II. The Series II cars had been redesigned to meet federal safety standards. The Series III, introduced in 1975, continues through the present. All Excalibur engineering is handled by Stevens's son David, who designed the current chassis from the ground up. The result is one of the best-handling American cars in production.

The 1979 Series III Excalibur phaeton and roadster are not sports cars. Instead, they are fast, extremely well-built, rather ostentatious touring machines. Long, sweeping, skirted front fenders flow into unskirted rear fenders, which are integral with the body. The spare tires are mounted on the front fenders in fiberglass shells. Both models offer a skirted, rear-mounted fuel tank. The cars *exceed* government safety regula-

tions—a tribute to the versatility of Excalibur Automobiles. Standard equipment includes four-wheel power disc brakes, chrome-plated wire wheels, leather upholstery, removable hardtop, self-leveling rear shock absorbers and literally any body color the customer wants.

Stevens says the Series III can cope with federal regulations through 1982. An interesting side project, apparently tabled, is a smaller, lighter Excalibur based on the Vauxhall-Chevette. For awhile, federal fleet mileage standards seemed to point to this model as a necessity. But Excalibur has since received a partial exemption from the economy requirements.

Although his present Excalibur hasn't changed much in its SSK inspiration, Stevens's plans are intriguing. The Series III, he says, "updates the image of the car from approximately 1928 to 1933, when the SS Mercedes line of cars was superseded by the 380K, 500K, and 540K." Does that mean the Series IV Excalibur will be based on the fabulous K Series Mercedes? If so, sports-car enthusiasts can look forward to a spectacular new automobile in the 1980s.

Excalibur Series I roadster

THUNDERBIRD

Ford Motor Co., Dearborn, Michigan

If it hadn't been for the Corvette, there probably would never have been a Thunderbird. Between 1946 and 1955, Henry Ford II transformed his company from a derelict outfit to General Motors' number one competitor. That change required a Ford answer to any new product thrust by GM. When word leaked that GM was working on a sports car, the Thunderbird project began in earnest.

Sports-car designs had, of course, existed on paper in Dearborn before the Corvette project started. There wasn't a stylist in Detroit who didn't doodle two-seaters whenever he got the chance. After a hard day of designing bread-and-butter sedans, sports cars were dessert. Every stylist hoped that, by some quirk of fate, management would decide to build a two-seater and that the design chosen would be his.

Franklin Q. Hershey, Ford Division design director, claims a significant role in the T-bird project. Once he caught wind of the Corvette, he says, he began working vigorously. "I took a fellow named Bill Boyer, and we had a room off the main studio, and we started working on a clay model," Hershey said in 1972.

Another story has the project starting in 1951, which seems awfully early for Corvette news to be leaking out of GM. This second T-bird origin story involves Lewis D. Crusoe, Ford Division general manager. A down-to-

earth, hardbitten financial type, Crusoe was not particularly interested in sports cars—only profits. He had retired after a solid career at General Motors in 1944, only to be drafted by Henry Ford II for the Ford rebirth in 1946. According to Allen Nevins and Frank E. Hill, authors of the trilogy considered to be the standard Ford history (*Ford: The Times, The Man, The Company*; *Ford: Expansion and Challenge, 1915-32*; *Ford: Decline and Rebirth, 1933-62*), Crusoe "possessed the most varied experience of any Ford executive except Ernest Breech, being expert not only in finance, but in purchasing, labor, sales, and business administration . . . above all he had the imagination to deal with the problems his new position presented." Crusoe was 55 when the T-Bird project started. He didn't have many friends because he was blunt, decisive and demanding. But he got results.

In October 1951, Crusoe attended the Paris Auto Salon with George Walker, Ford design consultant. It was a banner year. Jaguar was exhibiting its Le Mans-winning XK; Bugatti, its Type 101 revival attempt; a Spanish company, the Pegaso; Chrysler, its K-310; Buick, its LeSabre and XP-300. Crusoe inspected these sports cars with the jaundiced eye of a GM-bred profit maker. A glamorous two-seater, he said to Walker, was just the thing Ford needed to spark its

1955 two-seat Thunderbird

somewhat tarnished image. Walker called home, and the studios went to work.

Although stylist Bob Maguire seems to have done most of the work, the Thunderbird was a committee design. It survived the corporate process of review and revision. One suggestion—fortunately shouted down—was that it be a chopped and channeled version of the 1955 Ford. The big-car's design was locked up before the T-bird's and did influence its design in small ways: the general lines, interiors, and windshields of the two cars were similar. But the T-bird did not come with the garish lightning-bolt side chrome of the passenger cars, or their accompanying two-tone paint jobs. Even more remarkably, management asked for few of the design clichés of the era. Garish grilles, side scoops, excess chrome trim, and complicated taillight assemblies were all rejected.

One big-car carryover that didn't hurt the design was the large, round taillights which were topped by small chrome triangles (used for back-up lights in 1956). These were applied as much for cost reasons as for family resemblance. Ford's stylists hated them, but later admitted that they actually helped preserve the T-bird's strong fenderlines.

All Thunderbird project work took place within these basic design parameters: curb weight 2,500 pounds; 50-50 weight distribution; 100-plus mph top speed; and better acceleration than the Corvette. The performance requirement was no problem, since Ford planned to use its Interceptor 292-cid V8 which developed close to 200 horsepower.

Naming the new sports car was a chaotic process. The original working names were standard passenger car titles—Sportliner and Sportsman. (There had been a wood-trimmed Sportsman convertible from 1946 to 1948.) Then some brand-new names were suggested: Arcturus, Savile, Coronado, and El Tigre. "Thunderbird" was submitted by stylist Alden Giberson, who was reminded of the legendary Indian bird of his native Southwest. Everybody thought Thunderbird was perfect. Ford registered the name just in time: there was a near collision with archrival General Motors, which was planning to use Thunderbird on a Pontiac show car. The GM car was hastily renamed Firebird.

Throughout the T-bird's early development, there was indecision about its character. Should it be a real dual-purpose sports car, qualified for the track and therefore Spartan in street form? Or should it be more the boulevardier variety, like the Kaiser-Darrin? A boulevard sports car was what Crusoe selected. By mid-1953 Ford had been able to purchase and evaluate a Corvette: executives blanched at its lack of roll-up windows, its low-displacement six, and its funny stone-guarded headlamps. Ironically the '53 Corvette wasn't any more trackworthy than the two-seater Thunderbird. It just appeared that way to Ford.

Crusoe's stand on the side of luxury entailed several alterations that dismayed purists. Instead of a British-style, take-apart convertible top, for example, Ford engineers created a complicated lift-up affair, mounted on folding top bows. Planners also demanded a removable hardtop, for people who liked their sports cars snug. These and other similar changes added considerably to the car's weight. From the target 2,500 pounds, the Thunderbird progressed to 2,850 pounds for the first running prototype, and to 3,200 pounds for production models.

The first production T-bird left the line on September 9, 1954, and was announced to an enthusiastic press on September 23. Even in 1955 dollars, it was inexpensive: just $2,944 with three-speed manual transmission, or $3,122 with Fordomatic. The engine

1956 Thunderbird

AMERICAN SPORTS CARS: THUNDERBIRD

Rear view of 1956 T-Bird

produced 193 bhp at 4400 rpm with 8.1:1 compression and standard. shift; 198 bhp at 4400 rpm with 8.5:1 compression and Fordomatic. The 292 V8's bore/stroke was 3.75x3.30 inches, having been bored out from the 1954 Ford V8's 272 cid.

From the very beginning, the two-seat Thunderbird was popular. Though it did not sell well enough to keep Ford satisfied (design of a four-seater began in early 1955), it outsold Corvette in each of its three years. And it held its value. In 1961, for example, used-car price guides put the retail value of a 1955 Thunderbird at $1,500—against about $600 for other cars of similar age and original list price. Model year production—not enough to impress Crusoe—was 16,155 in 1955; 15,631 in 1956; and 21,380 in 1957.

The '56 T-birds were altered slightly. The 292 V8 was sold only with stick shift, and was rated at 202 bhp; models equipped with Fordomatic and overdrive used a bored and stroked (3.80x3.44-inch) 312-cid V8 which delivered 225 horsepower when used with automatic, 215 hp with overdrive. Also available in 1956 was a

power kit, consisting of a hot cam and twin four-barrel carburetors. Power-pack models developed 245 bhp, with about 30 foot-pounds of torque. The main exterior change for '56 was a built-in continental spare tire.

The 1956 Thunderbird was somewhat better balanced, by virtue of this exterior spare tire, and had a performance edge on the '55. As most observers agreed, it was not a "pure" sports car. Ford was disposed to accept this judgment, having waived the race-and-ride approach in 1953. *Car Life* magazine provided an accurate summation of the little T-bird's real character: "Although it can go much faster than a MG, run dead heats with unmodified Austin-Healeys or Triumph TR2s at speed, and whip a Mercedes 190SL in acceleration, the T-bird still doesn't qualify and the others do. However, to Ford Motor Company's eternal credit, the T-bird is not claimed a sports car. . . . Rather, the maker calls it a 'personal' car. Perhaps Ford is too modest because the T-bird (with the Corvette) is far closer to a real sports machine than any other production automobile built on this side of the Atlantic."

In 1957 Ford drastically restyled the car, adding fins—which were probably inevitable—and a big combination bumper-grille. Engineers also introduced the ultimate performance Thunderbirds. The 312-cid V8 engine could be ordered with a Roots-type supercharger, which helped to deliver a genuine 300 horsepower. With twin four-barrel carburetors, the horsepower figure was 270 bhp to 285 bhp. The "standard" 312 engine produced 245 bhp at 4500 rpm. The 312-cid engines were sold with either manual or automatic transmission. Restricted to the manual gearbox only was the smaller 292, which offered 212 hp at 4500 rpm—the "economy" set up.

The wide variety of 1957 power teams allowed the Thunderbird customer to order any kind of car he wanted. A supercharged 312 could achieve close to 125 mph and do 0-60 in well under 10 seconds. A standard-shift car with the 292-cid V8 could run a 0-60

1957 Thunderbird

1957 Thunderbird, last year of the two-seaters

sprint in 13 to 14 seconds, and exceed 100 mph.

The T-bird's sporty looks belied its brakes and conventional suspension. Care would have to be taken in pursuing, say, a well-driven Porsche 356 into a decreasing-radius turn. The Thunderbird's brakes tended to fade after two successive stops from any speed over 60 mph. Its handling, while better than any passenger car's, was spongy and suffered strong understeer. The Thunderbird's purpose was pleasant, stylish touring, however, and it accomplished that with ease. The car was also proof positive that Detroit really could build handsome cars in the middle 1950s, despite the garishness of some models.

By the end of the '60s, two-seat Thunderbirds were selling used at their original list price, and prices have climbed steadily since then. Nevertheless, it is still one of the best investments among American sports cars. If and when the inflated values of "instant collector's items" like Cadillac's Bicentennial Eldorado, start plummeting, the two-seater Thunderbird's value will resume growing. Supply is limited—50,000 cars were built, and perhaps only 10,000 survive—yet demand for T-birds is not strident and impatient, like that for Corvettes.

Collectors of two-seat Thunderbirds generally believe the 1957 model is the most desirable, followed by the 1955 and the 1956. This is an uncommon situation. Usually in a three-year run, the earliest model is the most highly prized. But the 1957 Thunderbird offers certain advantages which outweigh its faddish styling: it was the last of the line, since the four-seaters followed in 1958; it was available with the widest array of power teams, and was the hottest performing two-seater by far; and it benefitted from three years of development. It had wind wings, sun visors, excellent interior ventilation, and 12-volt ignition.

The 1958 and subsequent four-seat Thunderbirds furthered Ford's goal of producing a personal luxury car. They outsold the two-seaters by as much as five to

one. The nearest that Ford came to a sports car after 1957 was the 1962-63 Thunderbird Sports Roadster. This was the only time a company turned a four-seater into a two-seater, though there are dozens of examples of the reverse.

Providing the impetus behind the Sports Roadster was Lee A. Iacocca, then Ford Division car marketing manager (later president of Ford; now president of Chrysler). Iacocca, a heads-up sales executive, wanted to satisfy dealer demand for another two-seat Thunderbird—but not by eliminating the obvious appeal of the four-seater. The result—thanks to designer Bud Kaufman—was a fiberglass tonneau cover. This cleverly designed cover could be kept in place with the top up or down, and during the lowering and raising process. It fitted snugly over the rear compartment and rose to form twin headrests for the front passengers.

Thunderbird sports roadster, 1963

Mustang I, created in 1962

The Sports Roadster sold for $5,439 in 1962 and $5,563 in 1963—roughly $650 more than the basic T-bird convertible. Wire wheels and the tonneau cover were standard. The price premium made it relatively unpopular. Only 1,427 Sports Roadsters were built for the 1962 model year; 455 for 1963. In 1964 the tonneau and wire wheels were offered only as dealer accessories.

Even as Iacocca pushed development of the Sports Roadster, however, work was underway on a genuine sports car in the Ford Design studios. The result, introduced in October 1962, was the interesting Mustang I. A lot of people hoped this car would go into production.

The Mustang I was created by engineer Herb Misch, stylist Gene Bordinat, and product planner Roy Lunn. With production very much in mind, this trio avoided the outlandish dream-car approach. They planned to avoid head-on competition with Corvette by aiming for the 1.5- to 2.0-liter class, and an 85- to 90-inch wheelbase. Needing a quick prototype, Ford asked Trautman & Barnes, special builders in Los Angeles, to help. T&B used a multi-tubular frame with a stressed-skin aluminum body, and nonadjustable seats (to compensate, the pedals were adjustable). Misch created independent four-wheel suspension with wishbones and coil springs up front, wishbones and radius rods in back. Steering was rack and pinion, taken directly from the prototype Ford Cardinal (which later became the German Ford Taunus 12M). This steering gear provided nimble response—only 2.9 turns lock-to-lock.

The Mustang I was powered by the Cardinal 60-degree V4, which displaced 1927cc (bore/stroke

Functional interior of the Mustang I

GT-40, an all-out competition machine

90x60mm). This engine produced 90 hp in standard form. Misch added twin two-barrel Weber carburetors and a crossover manifold to boost output to more than 100 bhp. A Cardinal transaxle carried four widely spaced gear ratios, coupled to a 3.30:1 rear axle ratio. The Mustang I had a 90-inch wheelbase and was 154 inches long. Its light construction gave it a weight of only 1,148 pounds, so even with the modest V4 power plant it was a great performer. Speeds of up to 115 mph were possible.

The Mustang I interior was styled by Ford. The cockpit had a five-pod instrument layout which housed speedometer, tachometer, ammeter, and fuel and water gauges. The choke and horn button were located on the central console. The interior was plain, but was in keeping with the goal of low production costs.

Ironically, the Mustang I was killed off by the avid reaction of sports-car people. Ford brought it to the U.S. Grand Prix in October 1962, and Dan Gurney drove it around the track on a demonstration run. The crowd loved it, as did the automotive press. This was precisely what Iacocca was afraid of. Later he remarked: "All the buffs said 'Hey what a car; it'll be the best car ever built.' But when I looked at the guys saying it—the offbeat crowd, the real buffs—I said 'that's sure not the car we want to build, because it can't be a volume car. It's too far out.'" All hands then turned to the 1965 Mustang project—a huge success.

The demise of the Mustang I ended Ford's interest in sports cars, except for all-out competition machines like the GT-40 and captive imports like the Pantera. A Ford sports car was simply not practical in terms of the volume that Dearborn needed to justify its place in the corporation's line.

Cobra designed by Gene Bordinat

Ford J-Car prototype racer

GAYLORD

Gaylord Cars Ltd., Chicago, Illinois

Just after World War II, some millionaire playboys, responding to the sports-car boom brought about by MG and Jaguar, put their ample resources behind their own dream cars. As might be expected, the majority of these turned out to be ridiculous. They well attest to former automotive magazine publisher John R. Bond's dictum, "a little knowledge about cars can be dangerous."

The brothers Gaylord were different. Ed and Jim were millionaires, all right: their father had invented the bobby-pin, and had been smart enough to patent it. The Gaylords also knew automobiles. Their family had owned Marmons, Lincolns, and Pierce-Arrows. Their youth was spent with hot-rod Packards, Cadillacs and LaSalles. Speed engineers like Ed Cole and Andy Granatelli were their friends and collaborators. Granatelli built Ed Gaylord a Packard that was the fastest thing on wheels in downtown Chicago immediately after the war. Gaylord knew it was, and the police probably still have the records to prove it.

In 1949 Jim Gaylord—the visionary of the two brothers—met with Alex Tremulis, then head of the styling department of the ill-fated Tucker Corporation. Jim Gaylord just popped in to talk about cars, and the conversation lasted long into the night. Five years later, Tremulis was at Ford, and Gaylord was visiting him again. "Alex, I'm going to build the world's finest sports car, and I want you to style it," the young enthusiast said.

Tremulis was prevented from contributing by the characteristically dim view Ford takes of such freelancing, so he recommended Brooks Stevens of Milwaukee. Stevens, of Excalibur fame, had a great deal of experience in automotive design on both sides of the Atlantic. He expressed enthusiasm, and went right to work.

Jim Gaylord's concept involved a modern envelope body, with classic overtones. He wanted an upright radiator, and big headlights. The body would ride a 100-inch wheelbase, and come complete with a hardtop that would disappear into the trunk. Stevens suggested that the body be built by his associates at the Spohn Company in Ravensburg, Germany. The Gaylords hoped to introduce a finished prototype at the 1955 Paris Auto Salon.

The first Stevens proposal was wild enough to please any eccentric. It was a garish, finned affair with forward-jutting fenders and huge headlights—much too big, as Stevens recognized, to really complement the design. The most interesting features were "free-standing" front wheels. The entire tire was visible under a cut-out front fender. A two-tone panel swept back from the wheel, curving upward from the rocker panel to form the trailing edge of the door. The colors were Stevens' favorites: black overall; the side panel, light ivory.

Steven's drawings progressed into quarter-scale models and finally into a hastily built, somewhat crude

Brooks Stevens with production-ready Gaylord

prototype, just in time for the Paris show. Relatively few styling changes were made. The new headlights, though, were much smaller than the originals. The exposed front wheels remained, but the jagged cutout around them was cleaned up.

The Gaylord's retractable roof was ingenious. With the push of just one button, the deck lid lifted on a pair of electric supports. A chain drive pulled the top back into the trunk. The roof itself contained a recessed rear window and extractor vents for stale air. Ford stylists took many photos of this system, but the later Ford retractable was much more complicated than the Gaylord.

The car, loaded with luxuries, originally listed at $14,500. The spare tire was stored on a tray in a panel under the rear deck. When it was needed, it slid out on rails, then dropped to an upright position for easy removal. A vast array of instruments was displayed across the oriental-wood dash. Each instrument included a warning light to supplement the needle reading.

Jim Gaylord designed the very strong chrome-molybdenum tubular chassis, using coil springs and A-arms for the front suspension, and a beam axle with leaf springs for the rear. The suspension made extensive use of rubber; the passenger compartment was absolutely impervious to shock over rough surfaces. The original engine was a 365-cid Chrysler hemi V8 with four-barrel carburetor. Later Gaylord cars were fitted with Cadillac Eldorado V8s. The transmission was a modified Hydra-Matic. When the accelerator was floored, a downshift didn't occur until peak revs were reached in each gear.

The Gaylord weighed close to 4,000 pounds, but it behaved like a 2,000-pound Excalibur J. Runs from 0 to 60 mph averaged about eight seconds. Top speed was an easy 120. The car tracked smoothly through all kinds of turns from fast, level bends to decreasing radius corners.

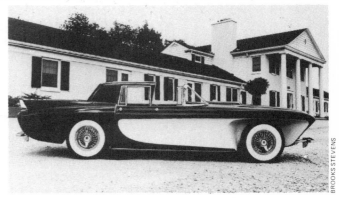

Mock-up of proposed four-door Gaylord

Yet the Gaylord failed. It was extremely expensive—the ultimate production price was $17,500—but that wasn't the real problem. Jim Gaylord was a perfectionist, and drove himself to a breakdown during the car's production engineering phase. Gaylord Motors also got into a quality dispute with the builders of the production car, Luftschiffbau Zeppelin in Freidreichshaven, West Germany. By 1957 the project had been abandoned. Three production chassis were built. Two of them are on display at the Early American Museum in Orlando, Florida. One chassis is bare, and is color-coded to indicate various components. It is almost more interesting than the whole car. The third chassis was left in Germany; its fate is unknown.

In retrospect, the main fault in the Gaylords' enterprise was the lack of solid production planning. The chassis—strong, capable, brilliantly designed—is worthy of any sports car ever built. The body, though it suffered from contemporary fads, was original and clean. It did not include such devices as tailfins and a wraparound windshield, so it still looks good today. It's a shame more Gaylords weren't made before the brothers gave up.

Original rendering for Gaylord

Ed and Jim Gaylord's ultimate sports car

KAISER-DARRIN

Kaiser-Willys Corp., Toledo, Ohio

Howard A. "Dutch" Darrin, alone among the custom coachbuilders of the classic era, survived the Great Depression and World War II to become an important force in postwar automotive design. In 1945 he was called on to create a new car for Kaiser-Frazer; he came back around 1948 to design the significant 1951 Kaiser. Along the way he built an intriguing fiberglass convertible, and proposed a sectioned Kaiser with 100-inch wheelbase for the K-F economy car. However, the company went with a different, unattractive design for the '51 Henry J Model. Darrin helped to smooth out its contours, but hated it with a passion—as did most of the public.

The Henry J had one thing going for it—a compact, conventional, well-built 100-inch-wheelbase chassis. Brooks Stevens used that chassis in building his potent Excalibur J, and Darrin used it to build his own unique sports car.

As soon as the Henry J had made its debut, Darrin went to work building his own body for it. "I realized," he said, "that its chassis deserved something better than it had received....I decided to make a sports car—without the authorization and knowledge of the Kaiser organization—spending my own money."

Darrin had never been satisfied with any car K-F built, even the ones he had conceived. Every time he

thought he had a design locked up, other stylists or engineers would do something to it that appalled him. In 1952, after his umpteenth break-up with Kaiser management for what he interpreted as meddling with genius, Darrin moved to Santa Monica, California. There he could work out his ideas, free of K-F's interference.

The possibilities of fiberglass had interested Darrin very early in his career. He was one of the first designers to campaign for its use in production. The sports car he developed, therefore, used a fiberglass body. The material was easy to work with, and lent itself to what Darrin knew would be fairly limited production.

Quickly, the Darrin sports car took shape. It was a rakish affair, with long, nicely curved front fenders dropping down to the traditional "Darrin dip" just ahead of the rear wheels. The rear fender swept up again, then tapered smoothly into a '52 Kaiser taillight. In side view, the Darrin was magnificent. It is still cited today as one of the outstanding automotive shapes of the 1950s, often by people who were Darrin's greatest critics back in '52.

The sports car did have several displeasing features. One was its sliding door mechanism. Darrin had been proclaiming the advantages of sliding doors since the

Original split-windshield Darrin prototype

Darrin prototype on display, 1953

early 1940s. He believed that conventional doors were clumsy and dangerous. In the sports car, which had long front fenders, there was ample room for the doors to slide when opened. Darrin mounted them on rollers, in accord with a patent he had filed. They slid three-quarters of the way into the hollowed-out fenders. In theory this was a good idea. In practice, the door opening proved too small, and the roller mechanism was found to be balky.

Darrin had never been pleased with the chromey, ostentatious grilles of typical 1950s automobiles. He was determined to make his sports car different. The result was a little rosebud grille, mounted in the center of the front end, capping the tapered hoodline. It was inadequate for radiator cooling, so Darrin included a wide scoop underneath the Henry J bumper. The grille remains the most criticized aspect of his car.

Darrin created a soft top having three positions—full-up, full-down, and midway. In the middle position, landau irons folded the front part of the top back; the rear section and windows remained in place for draft-free motoring. This workable concept was later adapted by British cars like Sunbeam and Hillman. On the Darrin prototype the hood mechanism disappeared into a one-piece decklid, which sprung up on steel struts. This left little room for cargo, however, so production cars had one compartment for storage of the top, plus a conventional trunk door.

In August 1952, Darrin decided that he'd progressed far enough to show the car to Henry J. Kaiser. The auto tycoon was not impressed. "Who authorized this?" he demanded. "We are not in the business of building

sports cars!" Darrin explained that the whole project was his own, and that he was prepared to build it independently of Kaiser-Frazer. That put things in a new light. Henry Kaiser ordered the sports car into production.

The story of the car's naming is the kind of comedy Detroit auto executives like to laugh about over cocktails.

Kaiser management felt the car should be called "DKF" for "Darrin-Kaiser-Frazer." Darrin became furious: "I said I couldn't imagine it. There was a DKF motorcycle, and a DKW car already....I said I had not signed over the designs to Kaiser-Frazer and would not under these circumstances." A big meeting was called at which all the heads of Kaiser Industries were present. "Each one of them voted for DKF," Darrin says, "except Henry's son Edgar, who remained silent. It looked like a landslide, until old man Kaiser softly said he hadn't voted! 'Oh Mr. Kaiser, surely we want you to vote,' came the reply. With a smile at me, Henry said, 'I vote we call it the Kaiser-Darrin—period.' "

Actually, "The Sports Car the World Has Been Awaiting" did carry the DKF-161 designation, but only as a model name. The formal debut of the prototype was at the Los Angeles Motorama in late 1952. The reviews were enthusiastic. But by the time the production engineers were finished with the car, Darrin was furious again. To satisfy the headlight height requirements of all 48 states, engineers bent the front fenders up, altering the low lines. Darrin asked them whether they'd ever heard of larger wheels—the height needed was only an inch or so extra—but apparently the idea

Darrin's three-position landau top

the Kaiser-Darrin used an F-head Willys six-cylinder engine. It displaced 161 cubic inches (bore/stroke 3.13 x 3.50 inches) and developed 90 bhp at 4200 rpm. The transmission was a Borg-Warner three-speed with standard overdrive. The rear axle ratio was 4.01:1 or 4.55:1, at buyer's option. Even though the car's fiberglass body was light, the power train did not make for a very hot sports car. The average 0-60 time of several road tests was about 15 seconds; top speed ranged between 96 and 100 mph. At least two early Darrins were experimentally equipped with superchargers, which probably should have been offered as an option. The blown cars could reach 60 mph in less than 10 seconds, and could easily exceed 100 mph.

In the sports-car world of 1954, the Kaiser-Darrin had some very powerful competition. The Corvette sold for about $150 less. Even with its standard six-cylinder engine, the Corvette was about four seconds quicker from 0 to 60 mph and had 10 mph more top speed than the Darrin. The V8 Thunderbird came later, but would have out-performed the K-D by an even wider margin. The Darrin was strictly a boulevard sports car. If a stock K-D was ever entered in an SCCA production race, nobody recorded the fact.

A relatively high price, a demoralized, dwindling dealer force, and a relatively small advertising budget almost killed the Kaiser-Darrin before it was launched. Toward the end of 1954, Kaiser-Willys dealers were selling Darrins for hundreds of dollars under list price, and the company was offering them in giveaway contests. Ultimately, only 435 were built, plus about a dozen Darrin-built prototypes which had split windshields and a lower fender line. More than 360 production cars have been discovered, along with one split-windshield prototype.

The Darrin wasn't quite dead after 1954, however. Dutch Darrin found 100 cars languishing in the company storage yards, and bought 50 to sell through 1954 at his Los Angeles showroom. Some of these he equipped with 304-hp Cadillac V8s. The Darrin V8s sold for $4,350 and had a top speed of about 140 mph. The Cadillac engine proved to be what the Darrin needed, and this version did race. Mrs. Briggs Cunningham drove one with success in SCCA competition. The car was fairly long and wide for trackwork, but then so was the Corvette. It seems certain that a serious production-racing effort, by a company in better financial shape than Kaiser-Willys, could have developed a reasonable competitor.

Several interesting Darrin-inspired ideas evolved from the production car. Kaiser stylist Herb Weissinger proposed a novel dual-cowl phaeton with four doors and twin windshields, which, of course, wasn't built. In 1956, Darrin himself got the sliding door to work two-ways—rolling into the front fender or the rear. He then conjured up an extended-wheelbase, four-place sports car, based on the Darrin and fitted with a Packard grille. He tried to interest Studebaker-Packard in it. Unfortunately, S-P in 1956 was roughly in the same financial shape as Kaiser was in 1954.

The middle 1950s was the time to buy a Darrin

had not occurred to them. Darrin went home angrily, and Kaiser went into production at its small subsidiary plant in Jackson, Michigan.

By this time, Kaiser-Frazer had bought Willys, and the car company had been renamed Kaiser-Willys. So

1954 Kaiser-Darrin

Kaiser-Darrin's doors slid into fenders on rollers

cheaply. A year after it went out of production, the 1954 K-D was priced at $2,175 by the used car industry. A 1954 Corvette was priced at $2,750. Prices never got much below that, but they held steady for another 10 years. By the late '60s, however, the price of good Darrins had achieved the original level. Throughout the '70s it has kept on increasing. Today, it's impossible to find one in any shape for less than $5,000. The price of a really good car can be twice that. One low-mileage original recently sold for $15,000. Considering price differentials this large, the Darrin may be one of those few American sports cars that are better bought for as little as possible, then restored from the chassis up.

The Henry J and Willys components make the mechanical phase of the restoration easy. And fiberglass responds better to restoration work than steel.

Driving a Darrin, while hardly a pin-you-to-the-seat experience, is a real pleasure. Handling can be excellent—better than that of the two-seat Thunderbird—and the ride is comfortable. The car looks good in motion or standing still. Since there are only 360 known, you won't be passing a look-alike very often on the road. Styling is a matter of personal opinion, but a lot of people think a Darrin looks better than a 1953-55 Corvette. In any case, it's a worthwhile investment whose value can only keep increasing.

Kaiser-Darrin with one-piece windshield, higher front fenders

KURTIS

Kurtis-Kraft Inc., Glendale, California

Racing-car builder Frank Kurtis claims to have produced America's first postwar sports car. From the 1920s through 1948, Kurtis made a name for himself with highly competitive stock-car-based racers—particularly midgets. He achieved even greater fame with a series of formidable Indianapolis cars which won the "500" four times between 1950 and 1955. Kurtis built his two-seater in 1948 and 1949, after his midget racer period and before his Indy successes. Frank Kurtis's vast experience in competition accounted for the light, strong and deceptively simple Kurtis Sport Car. It had, as *Motor Trend* said, "all the features a sports car should have: speed, maneuverability, acceleration, power and sleek looks." Although 95 percent of its mechanical components were stock production-car items, they were carefully packaged for maximum performance. Kurtis saw to it that all chassis factors—spring rates, shock absorber settings, weight distribution—were attuned to maximum roadholding and performance.

The Kurtis sports car had a 100-inch wheelbase, measured 68 inches wide and 169 inches long, and weighed only 2,300 pounds. Its chassis and body were integral: the frame longitudinals and cross members formed part of the body. Ten smooth but bulbous body panels were built over this supporting structure. The body was mainly aluminum, but it had steel doors and a fiberglass hood and deck.

Kurtis's simple bumper-grille was a forerunner of today's safety bumpers in that it was mounted on rubber shock absorbers. A chrome rub rail extended around the body, protecting the sides as well as the front and rear. A special removable hardtop with plastic side windows was fitted. The interior featured a full array of instruments, including a tachometer.

Into this tuned body-chassis Frank Kurtis first installed a supercharged Studebaker Champion engine. This small L-head did not respond as well as he had hoped it would, so he experimented with a variety of V8s. Ford flatheads with 110 horsepower were used in some cars; other Kurtises had 160-hp Cadillacs. These employed the new short-stroke Cadillac engine that was the prototype for all modern V8s.

With V8 power, the Kurtis was impressive. Wally Parks, then editor of *Hot Rod,* clocked 142.515 mph at Bonneville in a Kurtis fitted with an Edelbrock-modified flathead Mercury engine. John R. Bond of *Road & Track* was overwhelmed with the Cadillac-Kurtis's pin-you-to-the-seat power. He said he believed the car would outhandle a Jaguar XK-120.

But Kurtis's small factory was incapable of high production. A handful of cars—estimates are between 20 and 34—were built before Kurtis sold out to Earl "Madman" Muntz for $200,000.

In the later '50s Frank Kurtis again built a street/track sports car, the 500S. Based on his tubular-frame Indy racing cars, it had a Spartan, Allard-like body. Kurtis sold about 25 of the 500S cars at about $5,000 in 1954-55, before dropping them to concentrate on all-out competition machines. A few more cars, with smooth fiberglass bodies and Ford V8 power, were sold as the Kurtis 500M.

Frank Kurtis and his car

Kurtis 500S

MUNTZ

**Muntz Car Co., Glendale, California and
Evanston, Illinois**

Carl "Madman" Muntz had been a promoter since the age of 12, when he bought old Model Ts, fixed them up and sold them at a profit. He opened a used, car lot in his hometown of Elgin, Illinois in the early '30s. Later he began selling car radios. Through 1940, Muntz rapidly built a small sales empire. Just before the war, he moved to Los Angeles, and claimed he was the "world's largest car dealer." Everybody in LA knew the Madman. Shortly after the war he began peddling Muntz televisions ("Stop staring at your radio, folks!"), Kaiser-Frazer cars ("Buy a Kaiser and Surprise Her"), and used cars by the thousands ("I want to give 'em away, but Mrs. Muntz won't let me. She's craaazy!"). In 1949 he bought Frank Kurtis's customized Buick. The short wheelbase and rounded body of this car prefigured the Kurtis Sport Car. When Frank Kurtis decided to quit the auto business, the Madman bought him out. Muntz built 28 Muntz Jets in Glendale before moving the factory to Evanston, Illinois. There, another 366 Jets were built between 1950 and 1954.

The bizarre exterior of Earl Muntz hid the marketing savvy of a Barnum. Taking a careful look at the Kurtis, he instituted some changes to boost sales. As a two-seater, the Kurtis lacked broad appeal, so Muntz increased its wheelbase. The Muntzes built in Glendale measured 113 inches, and those built in Evanston, 116 inches, compared to the 100-inch wheelbase of the Kurtis. As quickly as he could, Muntz switched from aluminum bodies to steel, which was not only more durable, but cheaper. Muntz Jets sold for $5,000-$6,000. Equipment included Hydra-Matic transmission, a cocktail bar for the rear seat passengers, and a big Muntz radio mounted over the transmission tunnel.

Muntz also changed the engine specifications. Kurtis had been running a 3.73:1 rear axle ratio which, Muntz said, "would just unravel" the Cadillac V8. He installed a 3.24:1 rear axle that made the Jet a bit slower off the line than the Kurtis, but faster at the top end. According to Muntz, a Jet would do 128 mph. After the move to Illinois, Muntz made a deal with Ford and switched to flathead Lincoln V8s: 336.7 cubic inches, 154 horsepower. These heavy engines had an adverse effect on handling. Later Jets were hardly the ground huggers Kurtis Sport Cars had been. The difference between the Muntz and Kurtis was similar to that between, say, the Kaiser-Darrin and Arnolt-Bristol. The Muntz and Darrin were boulevard sports cars; the Kurtis and Arnolt were dual-purpose machines, highly competitive on the race track.

By no means, however, was the Jet unexciting to drive. Acceleration from 0-60 mph ran between 9 and 12 seconds; top speed was around 110 mph. The wider wheelbase and luxury equipment made it much heavier than the Kurtis—on the order of 3,800 pounds. Yet its performance was far better than any ordinary production car of that weight.

Muntz stopped building his sports car for the same reason as a lot of other custom car producers. He was losing money—about $1,000 per car, he says—through lack of volume. His overhead was high, his labor costs excessive. When he began having troubles in the television business, the relatively minor sports car operation was the first to go.

The last score of Muntz Jets had fiberglass fenders and 205 bhp overhead valve Lincoln V8s. Mechanical specification doesn't affect their price today. A good one sells for $5,000-$7,500. They are not pure sports machines like Kurtises, but they are satisfying to drive, and remarkably easy to maintain.

Madman Muntz's $6,000 Jet

The Jet--luxury and room for four

NASH-HEALEY

Nash-Kelvinator Corporation, Kenosha, Wisconsin

You could search a long time for a more unlikely combination than George Mason and Donald Healey. Big George made his mark in the appliance business, came to Nash before World War II by way of the Kelvinator annexation, and in 1945 replaced Charles W. Nash as company president. The first automobile he produced as head of the firm was the '49 Nash Airflyte, a balloon of a car that bore a close resemblance to an upside-down bathtub. Healey, the smiling Cornishman, never drove a bathtub in his life. An amateur mechanic turned rally driver, he'd won events like the Monte Carlo Rally for such diverse marques as Triumph, Invicta and Riley. Mason chomped on cigars and shot ducks in his spare time; Healey drove fast cars and, when he could drag himself out from behind the wheel, dreamed about his own automobile.

After the war Healey finally built a car himself. Using chassis and bodies of his own design, and a 2.5-liter Riley engine, Healey created a series of attractive sedans, roadsters, convertibles and coupes between 1946 and 1951. He built only about 500 of them, but 20 percent were "Silverstone" models. These light, fast, cycle-fendered two-seaters were brilliantly successful in European competition.

One racer who recognized the Silverstone's potential was Briggs Cunningham. In 1949, Cunningham dropped a Cadillac engine into one, along with a De Dion rear axle. He finished an impressive second in the 1950 200-mile Palm Beach, Florida, road race. The same year a Cadillac-Healey won the Seneca Cup 100-miler at Watkins Glen, New York, with Phil Walters driving.

Donald Healey met George Mason in late 1949, on a westward-bound voyage aboard the *Queen Elizabeth.* Healey was en route to the States where he hoped to open fresh markets for his cars. Mason was returning home from a European tour, fired up by the exotic

Original Nash-Healey, 1951

1953 Nash-Healey

sports cars he'd seen. A few drinks, a few cigars, and an idea hatched: why not build a Nash-based two-seater, powered by the big 3.8-liter (235 cubic-inch) Nash six? The result was one of the first Anglo-American hybrids.

The overhead-valve Nash six was a strong, modern unit capable of a fair amount of "hotting up," as Healey quickly found. He fitted it with a pair of British SU carburetors, a hot cam and an 8:1 compression aluminum cylinder head. The result was a healthy 125 horsepower at 4000 rpm. Healey combined the three-speed Nash transmission with Borg-Warner overdrive, and hammered out a racing body—a smooth envelope with a large headrest—and entered the car in Italy's Mille Miglia. It finished ninth in its class. For Le Mans, two N-Hs were entered and one of them finished fourth overall behind two Talbots and a Jaguar. A year later a lone N-H racer was sixth overall, and fourth in class. The cars had proved their mettle in the toughest endurance races ever devised.

The car's performance and durability established, Mason and Healey worked toward putting it into production. Aluminum bodies were built by Panelcraft Ltd. in England. Healey's company in Warwickshire built the cars; using his own roadster styling. For purposes of image, he bolted on a Nash grille, badge, headlights, bumpers and other trim parts. Production began in mid-1950; the car made its debut at the London and Paris shows in the fall and at Chicago in

February 1951. Early that year Healey was shipping 10 cars a week to the United States.

The 1951 Nash-Healey listed for $4,063, and standard equipment included an adjustable steering wheel and leather upholstery. The wheelbase was 102 inches and the car weighed around 2,700 pounds. It would have weighed more had the body been made of steel, but the weight wasn't excessive considering the healthy power plant. Nash sold 104 Healeys for the 1951 model year—not many, really, but worth a lot in publicity. By this time Nash had its hand in several interesting automotive pies. Besides the Healey and the big Airflytes, it was producing the compact Rambler, and working on the even smaller NXI, which became the Nash Metropolitan.

Big George Mason didn't care much for Healey's aluminum, slab-sided British body with its two-piece, flat-pane windshield. For 1952, therefore, the design work was farmed out to Pininfarina, which had just finished the all-new (and greatly improved) Ambassador and Statesman. Farina added the Italians' flair for smooth styling to the American components and British engineering, and the result was an extremely pleasing sports car. The headlights were mounted inboard, a two-bar grille between them; the windshield was one-piece and slightly curved; the rear fenders had a pronounced bulge, breaking up the slab sides. The body was now all-steel—cheaper and easier to repair than aluminum. By careful engineering, curb weight

AMERICAN SPORTS CARS: NASH-HEALEY

was actually reduced. The 1952 version sold for much more money: $5,868, but production increased to 150 units for the model year. In late 1952 Nash fitted a larger engine of 4.1 liters (253 cubic inches) displacement. The compression ratio was raised to 8.25:1 and Carter carburetors replaced the SUs. The larger engine developed 135 hp at 4000 rpm. This engine was fitted to most cars for 1953 and later.

Again in 1952, the Nash-Healey was entered in both the Mille Miglia and Le Mans. In the Italian race, a coupe driven by Donald Healey and his son Geoffrey crashed, but a second car driven by Leslie Johnson and W. McKenzie finished fourth in class, seventh overall. This was more significant than it sounds, because seventh in the Mille Miglia is like first in almost any other kind of event. Run over Sicilian roads, many of them more goat tracks than highways, it was a notoriously tough race.

But Le Mans '52 was really Nash-Healey's finest hour. Donald Healey entered two cars: an open sports model built over from the 1951 coupe, driven by Johnson and Tommy Wisdom; and the 1950 prototype, driven by Frenchmen Pierre Veyron and Yves Giraud-Cabantous.

In the general scheme of things, the Nash-Healey was no match for the fire-breathing sports racers of Ferrari, Jaguar and Cunningham. Le Mans strategy was always predicated on running a conservative race, waiting for the leaders to make mistakes and drop out. With the battle two-thirds over, the Johnson and Wisdom roadster was running sixth, behind two Talbots, two Mercedes cars, and an Aston Martin. The Veyron and Cabantous car had retired: it had an experimental cylinder head and was putting out around 200 horsepower, but it did not prove reliable.

Now Healey's strategy began to pay off. Around the 20th hour of the race, the lone Nash-Healey was fifth, passing one of the Talbots. Then, suddenly, the Aston Martin pitted with rear axle problems; the N-H was now fourth. The leading Talbot dropped out with engine problems. The N-H was now third. Alas, the two Mercedes didn't buckle, and they led the N-H across the finish line. But its third place overall was tremendously impressive, since the German cars were far more powerful. The Nash-Healey had averaged over 90 mph; hitting as high as 140 on the Mulsanne Straight. It handily won its class and finished second in the Index of Performance. Furthermore, it finished higher than any Ferrari, Talbot, Jaguar, Aston or Cunningham. And it delivered 13 miles per gallon and consumed no oil or water for the whole 2,200-mile running.

In the 1953 model year, 162 Nash-Healeys were produced. Also during 1953, a coupe model was added on a longer, 108-inch wheelbase. Probably the prettiest of all Nash-Healey cars, it was named Le Mans, in honor of the great 1952 performance, and won an award at the Torino Auto Show's custom body concours. Prices were now $5,444 for the convertible and $5,899 for the coupe. The convertible weighed 2,700 pounds in 1953, the coupe 2,970.

Hardtop models proved relatively popular, so in 1954 the convertible was dropped. The coupe was modified, as Nash switched to a three-piece wraparound rear window instead of the one-piece 1953 backlight, and the rear side glass was raked back at the top. A total of 90 coupes were built for 1954; some were left over and registered as 1955 models.

Donald Healey made one more assault on Le Mans with the Nash-Healey, but his emphasis in 1953 was

1952 Nash-Healey coupe designed by Pininfarina

1956 Rambler Palm Beach

on the new Austin-Healey 100-4, which he was producing in cooperation with the new British Motor Corporation. But two Nash-Healeys were also entered, one driven by the two Frenchmen; the other by Leslie Johnson and Bert Hadley. Again the French dropped out of the race, but Johnson and Hadley ran on to an 11th place finish at a 92.5 mph average

If the Nash-Healey had continued to evolve, the 1956-57 version might have looked like the Rambler Palm Beach—a sleek two-seater by Pininfarina on a wheelbase the same as the Nash-Healey convertible. The Palm Beach was more compact than the Nash-Healey, with an aggressive-looking oval grille, faired-in headlights, and tailfins at the rear. Its power, however, was supplied by a 90-horsepower Rambler engine, which was hardly in the same class with the big Nash-Healey engine. But more pressing concerns—chiefly substantial losses after the Nash-Hudson merger and the exigencies of separating the profitable products from the losers, prevented volume production of the Palm Beach.

Nash-Healey volume was not sufficient to warrant further funds for research and development. And Nash was losing about $2 for every $1 the Nash-Healey earned. Possibly the N-H would have been more successful if sold by specialist sports-car dealers: a Nash agency was the last place in which sporting motorists were likely to be found. But its price was stiff in relation to its competition—the Kaiser-Darrin, Chevrolet Corvette and, in 1955, the Ford Thunderbird.

Out of the 506 Nash-Healeys produced, over half are known to survive today, largely through the aegis of an enthusiastic Nash-Healey club. You can, if you like, own one of these modern thoroughbreds for not much more than a new Pinto, which ought to be enough to tempt the pocketbook of the frugal car lover. Beauty is in the eye of the beholder, of course, but to practiced eyes the original 1951 aluminum-bodied Nash-Healey looks purer, cleaner—if more slab-sided—than its successors. If this is your feeling, you're in luck, because the '51s sell for up to $2,500 less, car for car, than the 1952-55 models. One international price guide quotes $3,650 as the sale price of a 1951 in very good original condition, showing minor wear. In design, the major drawback of the 1952-55s is their queer inboard headlamps—but a good original car can cost $5,000, and one in show condition $7,500. The big advantage to the steel cars is their ease of repair. The aluminum-bodied '51s won't rust, but repair work will be extremely expensive.

Aside from the body differences, what we have here is a thoroughly simple, straightforward, easy-to-maintain automobile. Parts are in adequate supply and there is plenty of expertise available. Considering everything—driving pleasure, racing heritage, good styling, engineering and price—it's hard to think of a better buy for the money among vintage sports cars than a Nash-Healey. But with the supply limited, prices are on the move. Don't wait too long if you really want one.

SHELBY

Shelby-American Inc., Venice, California
Shelby Automotive, Ionia, Michigan
Ford Motor Co., Dearborn, Michigan

Carroll Shelby has become the hottest name in American sports cars. Every car with which he was associated is now considered a postwar classic—from the Cobra 289 to the Ford GT40, from the Cobra 427 to the Ford Mark IV. The problem with all these fabulous cars is that they were built in limited numbers—less than 1,000 Cobras, for example. And the prices reflect this. A good Cobra now costs at least $30,000.

One Shelby car is still a bargain for collectors, however. A decent GT-350 can be had for under $5,000, and though it is not as rare as the others, it has all the panache of the more expensive machines. There were 2,950 Shelby Mustang GT-350s built in 1965 and 1966: 562 in 1965; and 2,378 in 1966.

While Cobras are custom-built one-offs made by hand on what was laughingly called an assembly line, the GT-350s are hot-rodded Mustangs in the best

1968 Shelby GT-500

1966 Shelby GT-350

southern California tradition. *Car and Driver* tested one in 1965 and labeled it "a brand new clapped-out race car."

The GT-350 was designed to be used as an SCCA B-production racer, and it came from the factory capable of beating the 283 and 327 cubic-inch Corvettes which dominated B-production racing in those days. The GT-350 also filled a gap in Ford Motor Company's lineup of mid-1960s racing cars. In 1965, Ford fielded the Cosworth V8 in Formula One competition; the Indy-Ford for Indianapolis; the GT40 and Daytona coupe for international endurance racing; the Holman, Moody, and Stroppe Fords for NASCAR; Falcon Sprints and Mustang GTs for international rallies; and Cobras for A-production. The only gap to fill was B-production, and that's what the GT-350 was for.

The GT-350 did the job. In 1965, Jerry Titus of *Sports Car Graphic* won the B-production National Championship. In 1966 Walt Hane won it again in the same car, and in 1967 Fred Van Beuren won the championship in his GT-350. Mustang GT-350s also won dozens of smaller races, were turned into successful drag-racing machines, and made excellent rally cars. Considering its plebian origins, the GT-350 is one of the most successful sports cars ever. The fact that it worked is remarkable.

It takes some doing to make a real sports car out of a four-seater pony car that rides a Falcon chassis, so Carroll Shelby and crew obviously had their work cut out for them. Still, the easiest way to describe a GT-350 is to state how it differs from a stock Mustang.

There were always two different GT-350s: a street version barely removed from the race track, and a full-race version. This full-race GT-350 was one of the few production sports cars sold since the days of the

MG TC that was ready to race as you bought it.

Shelby started with the street version. This was necessary because the SCCA required 100 identical cars to be built within a year to make a model eligible for the production road-racing classes. But in the mid-1960s, the SCCA seemed unable to define a sports car, the Porsche 911 and Alfa-Romeo GTV epitomized cars: they were high-performance two-seat coupes that offered remarkable performance, handling and braking. But through a quirk in the SCCA rules, the Porsche 911 and Alfa GTV could be fitted with thin jump seats in the rear and be considered as "sedans" for Trans-Am racing. For about five years, both Alpha and Porsche raced the same cars in sports-car and sedan classes, and won handily in both.

This confusion worked to Shelby's advantage, too. The Mustang was obviously a sedan, and Trans-Am sedan racing was literally designed around the Mustang and its competitors—Camaro, Firebird, Cougar and Barracuda. Mustangs won the big sedan races throughout the late '60s. But the Mustang—at least in Shelbyized form—was also a sports car in the eyes of the SCCA. Since the SCCA took into consideration the number of passengers the car could carry, Shelby turned the Mustang into a two-seat sports car by removing the rear seat and mounting the spare tire on an empty shelf.

The Mustang that Carroll Shelby chose to turn into a sports car was the sleek fastback. It had a 108-inch wheelbase; and a partially unitized body-chassis with a subframe to carry the engine, transmission, and front suspension. Shelby ordered his cars from Ford painted all in white and fitted with the high-performance version of the 289 cubic-inch V8. He rated them at 271 hp in stock trim. Shelby added a high-rise manifold, a big

1969 Shelby GT-500

four-barrel carburetor, and a set of freeflow exhaust headers fabricated from steel tubing. The little Ford small-block, one of the great engines of all time, was capable of churning out 306 hp at 6000 rpm.

Borg-Warner's T10 four-speed transmission was the best unit available for purchase in 1965, and it was a factory option on any Mustang. Shelby naturally ordered it on all the cars he intended to modify. For street use, the T10 was strong enough, so it was left alone. However, Shelby's horsepower experts were preparing to dump more horsepower into the Mustang than Ford had ever imagined.

The Mustang used a Falcon rear axle, just strong enough in stock trim. Shelby replaced the entire rear end with one from a Fairlane station wagon. This provided a heftier center section, and 10 x 3-inch drum brakes which were better in every respect than the stock Mustang brakes. Metallic linings were the finishing touch.

The new rear axle was located with a trailing arm at either side. Koni shock absorbers supplanted the four stock units. The front suspension received more attention than the rear. For starters, all of Shelby's cars were ordered with the optional Kelsey-Hayes disc brakes that Ford offered for the Mustang. These were then fitted with metallic brake pads. By mid-1960s standards, these gave sensational braking.

To reduce the Mustang's terrible understeer, Shelby's crew shrewdly relocated the front suspension mounting points. In the Shelby version, handling became surprisingly neutral, and the tremendous power of the hot-rodded small-block Ford was more than enough to break the rear tires loose at any time. A huge front sway bar stiffened the whole arrangement. The most exotic and clever touch was a heavy steel-tubing brace that connected the tops of the front shock absorber towers to each other. On the stock Mustang, these relatively unsupported mounting points were free to flex independently under hard cornering. By simply bolting a length of tubing from one point to another, across the top of the engine itself, Shelby improved the car's handling immensely.

Shelby cast his own aluminum wheels with a big 15-inch diameter and 6-inch rims. The cars were fitted with wide, high-performance, Goodyear bias-ply tires, the best available prior to the invention of the domestic radial. Shelby also replaced the stock steering box with one that had a much quicker ratio. Not only did this give the GT-350 better handling, but it provided better *perceived* handling.

The outside of the GT-350 was as thoughtfully designed as the chassis. First, Shelby took the prancing pony out of the grille and left a simple oval. He replaced the steel hood with a fiberglass replica which was lighter, and included a smooth little hood scoop that soon became a Shelby trademark. This new hood was held on by NASCAR hood pins, for a race-track look. The stock Mustang had a carved-out section in the body sides, reminiscent of a Ferrari brake-cooling scoop. Shelby made it functional and used it to direct cool air to the rear brakes. These rear side scoops projected slightly from the stock body, but they gave the car a tough, racer appearance.

The stock Mustang fastback had a forced-air ventilation system. Air exited from small grilles set into the C-pillars. The 1965 Shelby cars did not alter these, but for 1966 models, the grilles were removed and replaced with plastic rear quarter windows. These improved rear visibility from the driver's seat, and made the GT-350 appear much lighter than the stock Mustang. When the bodywork was done, the finished car was given two wide blue stripes on a white background, or two white stripes on a blue background.

The interior of the GT-350 was only slightly different from that of the stock Mustang. The most obvious changes were the use of three-inch seat belts, a fancy steering wheel with a polished mahogany rim, and a full set of gauges set into unused space on the dashboard. All the GT-350s were ordered from Ford with black interiors, and surprisingly enough, the stock Mustang seats—uncomfortable as they were—were retained. Even more odd, after Shelby had removed the rear seat and replaced it with the spare tire from the trunk, he designed an optional kit to relocate the tire in the trunk and add a new-style rear seat cushion.

The full-race version of the GT-350 was basically the same car, but was fully prepped for the track. The engine was now a 350-hp 289 V8, lifted intact from the racing Cobras. Behind it was located a four-speed Warner gearbox, with an aluminum case to save weight. The interior was stripped and a real racing seat was installed. A mandatory rollbar and harness went on. Shelby would install a variety of other personalized performance parts for those buyers willing to pay the price.

A heavy suspension was bolted in. Genuine racing tires were fitted. The final touch was a whole new nose. Cast in fiberglass, it eliminated the front bumper, and provided a rudimentary air dam with a central slot that fed cooling air to an oil radiator mounted in the nose. Painted white and blue, these racing GT-350s looked surprisingly like the street machines, but they were quite a bit hairier. Later, some of these cars received four-wheel disc brakes, 400-hp engines, and really wide tires and wheels under flared fenders.

For $17 a day and 17 cents a mile—which was as expensive as rental cars got in 1966—you could try out a Shelby GT-350 owned by Hertz Rent-A-Car. Hertz bought 936 Shelby Mustangs and had them painted black with gold metallic stripes. The only differences between these cars and the custom GT-350s were the paint job and the transmission. Instead of the four-speed, Hertz ordered its cars with C-4 three-speed automatics and floor shifts.

Some of these cars were obviously rented on race weekends in towns like Watkins Glen and Lime Rock, to be returned on Monday morning with "B 43" or "B 77" painted on the doors inside white circles. Some enterprising racers, working with limited funds, rented one at Sebring in 1966 and put the Hertz car's engine into a Cobra as a replacement motor during the 12-hour race. Buying street-legal racing cars from Carroll Shelby was probably not the most profitable thing Hertz ever did, but the practice supplied collectors with almost a thousand GT-350s that otherwise wouldn't have existed.

In 1967 Ford Motor Company redesigned the Mustang into a larger, heavier car that was capable of accepting the 429-cid big-block V8. Shelby turned this new Mustang into the Shelby GT-350 and GT-500, with completely new fiberglass front ends, a lot of little styling modifications, and only small improvements to the chassis. These cars also cost about $4,500 in Shelby Mustang trim, but they should in no way be confused with the original GT-350s from 1965 and 1966. The earlier cars are blue-chip postwar collector cars; the 1967 and 1968 cars, which, although they bear the Shelby name, were actually produced in Detroit by Ford and are not considered to be as desirable as their predecessors.

Many people are collecting these later Shelby cars, and prices are as high as for the "real" Shelby GT-350s. The cars just aren't the same. If you're shopping for one of the wonderful products of Carroll Shelby, make sure the one you pick was really made by him in 1965 or 1966. The genuine GT-350s are the only ones which will hold their value in the long run.

1969 Shelby GT-500

WOODILL

Woodill Motor Co., Inc., Downey, California

The Woodill Wildfire was one of the first fiberglass sports cars. It arrived in 1952, a year or so before the Corvette and Kaiser-Darrin. But only a few were sold off showroom floors as completed cars. The bulk were kit cars, supplied to fit over conventional passenger car chassis. Most American sports cars of the postwar years were the brainstorms of individuals. The Woodill was no different. It was created by Woody Woodill.

Woodill was a prosperous Dodge dealer in Downey, California. In 1951 he learned about the Aero-Willys, Willys-Overland's first passenger car in 10 years and one of the best compacts of the '50s. Its 161 cubic-inch F-head six, while not the hairiest power plant ever created, was at least solid and reliable. Woodill enthusiastically acquired a Willys franchise to go with

his Dodge agency. The Aero could easily be, he thought, the basis for a sports car. (Brooks Stevens thought the same thing, and created the Willys-engined Excalibur J; Dutch Darrin used the Willys six in his sports car.)

Woodill was already interested in California's growing fiberglass body building business. One of the leading firms was Glasspar. Bill Tritt, one of Glasspar's principles, had designed a sleek roadster body for 100-inch wheelbases. Woodill contacted Tritt and the two agreed to produce a special body and chassis. They would use Willys components: engine, drive train, front and rear suspension. They had to create their own chassis, because the Aero-Willys had a unit body-chassis. They agreed that the resultant sports car should not sell for more than $3,000.

Fiberglass Woodill Wildfire, 1952

Woodill chose the name Wildfire for his two-seater (later he marketed a downsized child's version whimsically named Brushfire). He targeted it to make its debut at the 1952 Los Angeles Motor Show. Its frame was constructed on a 101-inch wheelbase by hot rodder Shorty Post. It featured a very low drive shaft tunnel, and a passenger compartment/firewall built into the frame. Post resisted his inclination to modify the Willys engine. It produced 90 horsepower and came with a three-speed overdrive transmission as standard. Woodill offered no fewer than nine rear axle ratios, ranging from a stump-pulling 5.88 to a conventional 3.88:1. Post reduced the steering ratio to only 2.5 turns lock-to-lock. The price of the assembled car was $2,900. Woodill recruited a network of Willys dealers to sell the Wildfire across the nation.

Woodill was market-wise, and soon realized that the conservative little Willys six was not enough for some drivers. So he had Post design the frame for use with Ford V8 chassis and drive train as well. These V8 models were apparently not considered Wildfires. Accounts of the day indicate that the Post frame used suspension and axles from the transverse-spring Ford models; and new Ford/Mercury flathead V8s and transmissions, mounted well back to achieve optimum weight distribution. With the dozens of bolt-on perform-

ance modifications then available for the flathead Ford, these cars had to be considerably faster than the standard Wildfire. But even a Willys-engined Wildfire weighed only 1,500 pounds, and was a veritable rocket off the line.

Glasspar's body was the Wildfire's best feature. It had a low, crouching silhouette, and a large oval radiator opening which accepted various kinds of grilles. Early models had vertical-bar grilles; later models used a black mesh or a simple bar from the Aero-Willys. At the rear, the fenders kicked up and were rounded off. They'd been designed to accept the good-looking Aero-Willys taillights. The first windshield was a two-piece affair which used flat glass panels; the later version used a single piece of curved glass. Typical, apparently, of all Wildfires, was an exterior spare tire. The gasoline filler pipe extended directly out of the stern, so it doubled as a tire holder and tank cap; the spare was held in place by a knock-off wire wheel hub which was also the fuel cap. Wildfire wire wheels were fakes. They were in fact wheel covers, bolted to standard steel wheels.

Wildfire interiors were apparently ad-libbed, because few are the same. One model used a wavy gull-wing type fascia containing four major gauges: a Willys combination speedometer, fuel gauge and tempera-

Woodill Wildfire with special Glasspar Body, mock wire wheels

AMERICAN SPORTS CARS: WOODILL

ture gauge; a 1949-50 Kaiser clock; a combination rev counter and vacuum gauge; and a German-made acceleration gauge to measure grades, braking forces and G-factors. In addition, the car had two minor gauges for oil pressure and amperes.

No provision had been made for standardized side curtains and top. California was the Wildfire's main market. Perhaps that's why Woodill left decisions about weather protection to the individual owner. One Wildfire owner, Louis Keefer, constructed a top from Triumph bows and adapted the side curtains from an Austin-Healey. He also redesigned the seats because headroom was insufficient with the top up. The Wildfire was more a backyard production than a manufactured automobile.

The Woodill Wildfire received tremendous publicity, appearing in most of the auto buff magazines. (Its slogan, "The 14 Hour Sports Car," referred to assembly time for kit versions.) It was also used in the movies "Knock on Wood," "Written on the Wind," and "Johnny Dark." The car came close to volume production. Willys-Overland was interested, and negotiations for production of the Wildfire by the Toledo firm were well along when Kaiser-Frazer bought Willys. K-F went on to build the Darrin, and Woody Woodhill went on selling Wildfires himself—assembled or in kit form.

The Wildfire kit cost between $1,000 and $1,200.

The fully assembled cars originally sold for $2,900. Later, the price rose to $3,263, and finally to $4,500. Between 1953 and 1956, Woodill says he produced 300 cars, of which only 15 were "factory assembled." Kit buyers could build a car at home for about $2,000, so the savings to those who were handy with tools could be substantial.

Glasspar, Woodill and other kit-car builders eventually packed up. Competition from completely assembled $2,000-$2,500 sports cars like Triumph and MG was considerable; and domestic models from Kaiser, Chevrolet, Nash and Ford also took sales from Woodill. Woody Woodill then took a Wildfire on a world tour, trying to interest South American and Australian government officials in a "universal car." He nearly succeeded in Australia.

Today, a Wildfire can be purchased for between $1,000 and $8,000, depending on its condition. The fiberglass body of the car is easy to repair; the Ford, Willys (and occasional Buick) mechanical components are plentiful. The car is a bolt-bucket over the road, but its performance and fuel economy are excellent. It's noisy, hard-riding and a bit loose at speed, but a lot of other sports cars were that way in the early '50s. Certainly the Wildfire is an interesting, good-looking, rare two-seater that played a key role in the development of the American sports car.

Aero-Willys taillights and bumper on Woodill Wildfire deck

AMERICAN SPORTS CAR SHOWCASE 2

More spirited, flashy automobiles
—one-offs, dream cars,
and production models—some
conceived and designed for the road,
some for the racetrack.

1954 Kaiser Darrin

1954 Kurtis 500S

1968 Ford-Shelby Mustang GT 500

1965 AC/Ford Cobra 289

1967 Ford Bordinat Cobra

Shelby-designed Ford GT40 racing car

1960 Plymouth XNR

1954 DeSoto Adventurer II

1953 Cadillac LeMans

1954 Corvair

1958 Corvette XP-700

1953 Oldsmobile Starfire

1954 Oldsmobile Cutlass

1956 Oldsmobile Golden Rocket

1956 Pontiac Club de Mer

CHRYSLER

Chrysler Corp., Highland Park, Michigan

1950 Dodge Wayfarer

Chrysler's distinguished line of sports cars and grand-touring dream cars was fostered by its chief designer, Virgil M. Exner, who headed Chrysler styling throughout the 1950s. Exner was a classic-car enthusiast who felt that the best designs of the golden age should influence modern automobiles. He viewed good styling as a combination of the best elements of the "British traditional, French flamboyant, Italian simplistic, and German functional" schools. He also had some close connections at Ghia coachworks in Torino, Italy. Thus Ghia built and helped design nearly all the Chrysler dream machines.

Exner's first project was the Chrysler K-310—more a grand tourer than a sports car. Mounted on the long, 125.5-inch Saratoga wheelbase, it ran the standard 180 hp FirePower hemi-head V8, and seated four people. True to Exner's classic themes, it had a bold, upright grille and fully exposed wire wheels. Its "gunsight" taillights prefigured those of the 1955 Imperial. The K-310 was a smooth, good-looking coupe that helped Chrysler overcome its reputation for dull styling, and, it came fairly close to volume production. But financial problems prevented the K-310 or a derivation of it from being offered to the public.

A number of show cars descended from the K-310. These can legitimately be labeled grand tourers. They were designed for fast pleasure driving more than for

the dual function of sports cars. They included the C-200, a K-310 convertible model; and a pair of Chrysler Specials built in 1952 and 1953 for corporate brass, the 1953 D'elegance (the spelling is Chrysler's), and the 1954 GS-1. The GS-1, mounted on a standard New Yorker wheelbase, went into limited production: 400 were run off by Ghia and sold through Chrysler-Europe's distributor in Paris. The D'elegance, on a very short wheelbase, saw 25 copies. It was significant as the direct styling forbear of Volkswagen's popular Karmann-Ghia, which VW liked to tout as "a Volkswagen by an Italian designer." In reality, the D'elegance, which anticipated every K-G feature except the grille, was created right in Detroit by Exner and his stylists.

The first Chrysler special with any claim to the sports-car title was the DeSoto Adventurer I of 1954. A striking coupe on the shortest dream-car wheelbase yet—111 inches—it was a compact four-seater that looked fast and *was* fast. Its engine was the DeSoto hemi-head V8. The car was fitted with a full set of instruments, exterior exhaust pipes, a racing type quick-fill fuel cap, and brake-cooling wire wheels. The Adventurer I also came close to production, as it was Exner's personal favorite. "If it had been built," he said, "it would have been the first four-passenger sports car made in this country. It was better than a 2 + 2, and of

81

DREAMS FROM DETROIT: CHRYSLER

1951 Chrysler K-310

1953 De Soto Adventurer

course it had the hemi engine. . . I owned it for three years and kept it at home." Though several Exner-Ghia show cars have survived, the Adventurer I has disappeared without a trace. "I think it eventually went to a wealthy collector in South America," Exner said.

The Adventurer I got Exner's sports car blood up, and subsequent Chrysler Corporation dream cars were generally short-wheelbase models with race-and-ride potential. The first of these was the Dodge Firearrow roadster, which influenced Gene Casaroll when he developed the Dual-Ghia. The initial Firearrow was a non-runner on a standard Dodge chassis; the second had an engine and ran quite well. A Firearrow coupe derivation achieved 143.44 mph on the banked oval of the Chrysler proving grounds.

While Exner toyed with his Dodge sports cars, Ghia had another idea: the DeSoto Adventurer II. Far different from the first Adventurer, it was a luxury coupe that rode on the standard 125.5-inch wheelbase. Exner had little to do with the design, though it followed the tradition of its predecessors: it was big and full-fendered, and had a prominent, blunt grille. Its super-

structure was semi-fastback. The automobile was a very graceful affair. Another predominately Ghia-inspired experiment was the aggressive-looking Plymouth Explorer, which had a bold, blunt vertical-bar grille that wrapped under the front of the body.

Plymouth dabbled twice in sports cars during 1954, hoping to compete with the Chevrolet Corvette and forthcoming Ford Thunderbird. Like Chevy, Plymouth engineers seriously considered a fiberglass body. To prove its feasibility, Plymouth built the 1954 Belmont. Sleek and very low, with pronounced fenders front and rear, the Belmont measured only 33 inches from ground to beltline. It used a Plymouth 114-inch-wheelbase chassis and was carefully designed for easy translation into a production model. A standard chassis with only slight modifications, Plymouth said, made possible the combination of "striking sport car smartness with a chassis design that has been proven in billions of miles of owner use." But no one ever suggested a stock Plymouth chassis for a road course. The azure-blue Belmont must therefore be considered a public interest tester rather than a genuine sports car.

Chrysler Fight Sweep II

1955 Chrysler Falcon

It is also one of the few Chrysler dream cars of this period that was designed without any input from Virgil Exner.

To Exner, the Belmont was an unlikely sideshow; he was far more concerned with his new Chrysler Falcon—a car that came as close as a Chrysler ever would to threatening Corvette.

In designing the Falcon, Exner shunned conventional chassis and went all-out to create a real sports car: he used a 105-inch wheelbase and a strong steel two-seat body. The Falcon was light and clean with minimal overhang. It was a thoroughly practical design. Power came from the efficient, 170-hp DeSoto hemi V8, so performance was adequate. Unlike many other Chrysler dream sports cars, the Falcon was finely attuned to both road and track. A CONSUMER GUIDE® magazine contributing editor has driven one of the three Falcons built. It is now in the hands of a collector. Although he was prevented from full acceleration workouts by a vague automatic shift linkage, we were told that the chassis was beautifully balanced, the steering smooth and precise, and the handling superb.

The Falcon's styling was as impressive as its engineering. The car had a purposeful look. It had an admittedly cramped interior, a short windshield, and a low convertible top. Up front was a large, blunt, Exner-type egg-crate grille; inset headlights; and prominent, creased fenders. The fenders ran back along the rounded fuselage, coming to modest rounded fins at the rear.

The Falcon bristled with thoughtful design features: taillights integrated with slim vertical bumpers; a gas cap cover built inboard of the left rear taillight housing, with a hole for pulling it open and a catch-ring to eliminate fuel spills; a beautiful, no-nonsense dash with a big speedometer and tach, and minor instruments arrayed to their right; and a small-diameter racing steering wheel. It's a shame that the Falcon never reached production, and sadder still that Chrysler let Ford have its glamorous name for an unassuming compact.

Two more sports cars from Chrysler drawing boards in 1955 were the Flight Sweep I and II: the former was a convertible; the latter a coupe. These were much

DREAMS FROM DETROIT: CHRYSLER

1960 Plymouth XNR

busier designs than the graceful Falcon, with prominent fins, clamshell-type front fenders, and Exner's dubious spare tire outline on the deck. The Flight Sweeps were exercises in design more than practical sports cars. They ushered in the radical, sometimes disconcerting, finned styling of production cars from 1957 and later. They were pretty automobiles in the context of 1955, but compared to the Falcon they appear dated now.

From 1955 to 1960, Virgil Exner shifted to larger chassis and specialized design efforts not connected with sports cars. But he was not quite through with proposals for two-seaters. In 1960 he created what many regard as his finest work—the radical and imaginative Plymouth XNR, with what Exner called "Asymmetrical Styling."

Exner's idea here was to emphasize the off-center driver's position, as did many racing cars. A prominent hood scoop was faired into the windshield and cowl, forming a headrest and tailfin behind the driver. The combination grille and bumper formed a large oval, and a perimeter bumper surrounded a mesh that contained the headlights. The passenger seat was covered by a metal tonneau when it was not occupied; otherwise, a small auxiliary windshield popped into place. It was "the first operational car ever built which so drastically altered accepted car styling by putting the streamlining features off center," Chrysler said. "This has been done because the driver's head and shoulders would project into the wind on such a low car, were it not for the compensating airscoop and stabilizer. To keep the passenger below wind resistance level, the passenger seat is four inches lower than the driver's. . . . Overall shape of the . . . . silhouette, is that of a single fin."

This breathtaking Plymouth sports car rode a 106-inch wheelbase, was 195 inches long, and measured 43 inches from the ground to its top of the rear fin. Its power came from a Valiant 225 cubic-inch slant six, but the engineers got it to produce upwards of 250 horsepower. "We took it to the proving grounds and had a professional drive it," said Exner. "He lapped at 151 or 152, which wasn't bad for that time." It isn't bad anytime!

What particularly excited sports-car fans was the XNR's efficient, economical six-cylinder engine—the first instance of a peformance six from Chrysler. It would have been suited to a sports car and capable of successful competition in its displacement class. Unfortunately, Chrysler decided that the XNR was too radical to build. Exner's departure from the corporation in 1961 prevented the car's refinement into a more practical model. A derivation, the Valiant Assimetrica, was later done up by Ghia, but it had none of the XNR's flair and never evolved beyond the prototype stage. The XNR itself still exists, though its whereabouts may be hard to document. It was last seen being driven by a sheik in Kuwait.

It is particularly unfortunate that none of the exciting Chrysler sports cars of the '50s and early '60s emerged into a product we could all buy. All you have to do is contemplate the light, sleek styling of the Adventurer I, Falcon and XNR to imagine how wonderful they would have been as production sports cars. Fortunately, quite a few of the limited-production specials have survived, and occasionally one comes up for sale. Most common is the GS-1, the highest-volume model, but prices are formidable. Chrysler enthusiasts are still searching for the K-310, the Adventurers, Plymouths and Dodges. Meanwhile, their companion models remain to represent the legacy of Virgil Exner.

GENERAL MOTORS

**General Motors Corp.,
Detroit, Pontiac, Lansing, and Flint, Michigan**

General Motors built a variety of Buick, Cadillac, Oldsmobile and Pontiac sports cars in the 1950s and early 1960s. Some were based on the Chevrolet Corvette; others were original dream cars having radical styling or sensational mechanics.

Among limited GM editions, Buick led the way. Its first dream car was Harley Earl's glamorous Y-Job of the late 1930s. Often displayed, modified and improved over the years, the Y-Job was finally relegated to the Sloan Museum in Flint in 1949. By then, it had forecast many Buick styling features of the late 1940s.

The Y-Job's successors were two really exotic machines, the XP-300 and the Le Sabre. These were developed by Earl's stylists and Charles A. Chayne, Buick's chief engineer. Because of his solid position in the GM hierarchy, Chayne was allowed to style the XP-300 independently of Earl, who handled the Le Sabre.

The Buick Le Sabre rode a 115-inch wheelbase; the XP-300, a 116. Both used unit bodies with frames of chrome-molybdenum box-section steel. Both had independent front suspension including torsion bars and ball joints, and a De Dion rear axle with coil-spring suspension. The brakes were jumbo drums that measured 9 x 3.5 inches. They were finned and centrifugally cast with double sets of shoes. The rear brakes were mounted inboard, like those of European racing cars. The front brakes were ventilated by air passages built into the grille and body sides.

The most astounding feature of the cars was the experimental aluminum V8 engine. It displaced 215 cubic inches, and was exactly square (bore/stroke 3.25 x 3.25 inches). Designed to prove what could be done with an unlimited budget and ultrahigh-octane fuel, it had 10:1 compression and developed a nearly unbelievable 1.5 horsepower per cubic inch—a figure that compares favorably with modern racing engines. This power was achieved by a Roots-type supercharger, and a fuel system that relied on a combination of gasoline and methanol. GM never revealed exactly how fast the two cars were. But they must have been capable of astounding performance.

Cadillac, too, produced a few sports cars in the 1950s—with little intention of mass production. Cadillac's market was well-heeled buyers of luxury cars. Earl and others argued that a two-seater would entice sporting customers, but management disagreed. The sportiest production Cadillac of the decade was the big Eldorado, which was hardly competitive on any racetrack.

Nonetheless, Cadillac's four sports cars were interesting, and worthy of mention. The first of the breed

Harley Earl's radical 1951 Buick Le Sabre

Buick Wildcat I

DREAMS FROM DETROIT: GENERAL MOTORS

Wildcat II, precursor of 1954 production models

Cadillac Le Mans, 1953

Olds F-88 Mark II

was the 1953 Le Mans—a bizarre concoction. From the cowl forward, Le Mans prefigured the 1954-56 Cadillacs. It had a big, chrome grille, "Dagmar" bumper guards, and hooded headlights. The Le Mans rear end, too, was a fairly accurate prediction of 1954-56 production-car lines. None of these details was particularly bad for the time. What spoiled them was the truncated two-seat body and short 115-inch wheelbase. These made the car look like a canary with eagle feathers. Surprisingly, Le Mans handled fairly well. Since its body was built entirely of fiberglass, the car responded vigorously to the stock 250-horsepower Cadillac V8. One magazine called Le Mans "too heavy and spongy for competition," thereby missing the point: Cadillac intended no competition; just a tidbit to interest showgoers.

For the 1954 GM Motorama, Harley Earl came back with two more integrated sports cars, La Espada and El Camino—a convertible and a coupe. These were basically identical and were built like Le Mans, but on a shorter wheelbase. They featured front and rear styling that would be seen on Cadillacs in 1957-59, but the look of both cars was more restrained, and therefore more acceptable, than the styling of Le Mans. Enthusiasts responded favorably. *Road & Track* had called Le Mans "that thing," but considered the two new cars "beautifully done." They were interesting in that they showed what the American sports car would have become had Cadillac produced it.

The last Cadillac special that could be called a sports car was the Cyclone of 1959. A steel-bodied two-seater on a 104-inch wheelbase, it was the shortest Cadillac in 50 years. Styling was of the twin pontoon type. There were sliding doors, and a plastic canopy hinged at the rear. The canopy swung open as the doors slid back. Powered by the standard 325-horsepower Cadillac engine which featured low-profile carburetor, cross-flow aluminum radiator and twin fans, the Cyclone was lightening quick. But again, it was not planned for production. Its most novel mechanical feature was a proximity warning device. Two aluminum reflectors mounted behind the pointed "nose cones" were connected to a transmitter and receiver in the front fenders. They sensed objects ahead by bouncing sound waves off them, warning the driver by means of lights and sounds that intensified as the distance decreased.

In Lansing, the "experimental division of General Motors" was experimenting. Oldsmobile's first sports car was the low and sleek 1953 Starfire, named after the Lockheed Starfire jet fighter. Like its contemporary, the Corvette, the Starfire had a fiberglass body. It also had a special 200-hp Rocket V8 engine. Like the 1953-54 Cadillac Specials, its role was to display future styling trends of production models. Its side styling and wrapped windshield showed what people could expect from Olds in '54; its grille was similar to the production grille of 1956.

In 1954 Oldsmobile came up with a sports car very much like the Corvette itself. The F-88, "a beautiful dynamo on wheels" was built of fiberglass, and had a

250-hp engine. Its design was much like that of the 1956 F-88 Mark II, which made use of the concave wheel well cut-outs that Harley Earl liked so much. A similar design appeared simultaneously on the production 1956 Corvette. These two F-88s would have been the total performance versions of the Corvette had they been put into production. But the Chevrolet sports car was hardly breaking any sales records, and GM decided to leave it unchallenged in its field. The first two F-88s, therefore, served only to whet the public appetite for things to come in production Oldsmobiles.

Just as it was introducing the first F-88, Oldsmobile was fielding an exotic experimental coupe, the Cutlass. Built on a 110-inch wheelbase, it featured a slotted backlight built into the semi-fastback roofline, sharply pointed tailfins and a scoop-type grille. Its novel features were seats that swiveled outward as the doors were opened, and copper-toned glass to cut down on glare. Swivel seats never made it into production at General Motors, but Chrysler introduced them as an option in 1959. (Chrysler stylists attended the GM Motoramas.)

Derived from the Cutlass but more radical yet was the 1956 Oldsmobile Golden Rocket, the Motorama counterpart to the F-88 Mark II. This low, aerodynamic rocket was built of fiberglass, with a split backlight not unlike that of the 1963 Corvette Sting Ray. Short, truncated fins rose behind the door openin and ended well forward of the tapered tail. At the front and rear of the Golden Rocket were sharply pointed cones, emphasizing its aircraft-derived styling. As the doors were opened, panels cut in the roof lifted, and the seats swiveled out. Even the steering wheel swung out of the way, as in the 1961 Thunderbird. The Golden Rocket would have made an impressive, though expensive, production sports car. But again, it was strictly an exercise.

In 1958 and 1959 the Earl studios progressed through two more generations of the F-88. The 1958 Mark III was a metallic blue roadster with updated styling from the Mark II. The Mark IV, painted bright red, was entirely new. Mounted on a 102-inch wheelbase, it was the prettiest F-88 ever. From the side it had a smooth cigar shape, uncluttered by chrome gewgaws. The body sides were curved. Extractor vents were sculptured in behind the wheels. The hood was long, extending ahead of the quad lights into an oval snout. The roof disappeared completely into the rear compartment at the touch of a button. This was the last GM show/sports car designed by Harley Earl. He liked it so much that he took it with him when he retired in 1959.

After the F-85 compact appeared in late 1961, Bill Mitchell began work on a sports derivation called X-215—a special convertible with fiberglass tonneau cover incorporating a roll bar. The X-215, one in a long line of experimentals, was shown at the Chicago auto show. A short, wind-cheating windshield, racing stripes, and roll bar gave it the look of a track contender. Again GM decided that it would remain only a dream machine. It was the last Oldsmobile show

1954 experimental Olds Cutlass

1956 experimental Olds Golden Rocket

Pontiac's Bonneville Special

Pontiac Club de Mer

DREAMS FROM DETROIT: GENERAL MOTORS

Prototype X-215

Corvair Super Spyder

vehicle that could conceivably be called a sports car.

Pontiac was active only briefly in the sports-car field, building the Bonneville Special in 1954 and the tailfinned Club de Mer in 1956. The Bonneville was a high-powered Corvette-like fiberglass two-seater with an ugly grille and faired-in headlights. The Club de Mer, a more daring exercise, introduced the dual-cockpit theme for driver and passenger and had a large sprung front end in place of a conventional bumper. Small two-seaters were not, however, Pontiac's forte. The division soon turned its attention to conventional-size performance cars, work that culminated in the GTO of the middle 1960s.

At Chevrolet, a sports car was already in production by 1953. Chevy also built a one-off, the '54 Corvair—a Corvette-based show car. In 1960, Chevrolet used the Corvair name on its production compact, powered by a 2.6-liter pancake six. Chevy and others built many Corvair specials. John Fitch put one into production.

GM found that turbocharging the Corvair engine would produce an easy 150 horsepower, along with 210 foot-pounds of torque at fairly high rpm. Numerous specials were built around this engine—notably the 1962 Super Spyder, a two-seater designed by the Mitchell studio. The SS used a conventional body, though its deck was lengthened by extending it forward. The deck ended in a pair of twin headrests behind the twin bucket seats. Other versions, both open and closed, followed, but none ever reached production. In 1962 Bertone built the beautiful Testudo, an ultralow fastback which appeared at the Geneva show in March 1963. Its most novel feature was a roof that flipped up to admit passengers. That idea was not new to Bertone, however; GM had designed a similar feature into the gorgeous Monza GT, which was shown in the U. S. during 1962. More conventional, but still very attractive in its own right, were Pininfarina's experimental Corvair coupes on conventional and short wheelbases. One of these survives and is on display at the Pininfarina Museum in Turin.

The Yenko Stinger was the name given to a Corvair-based sports car built by Don Yenko, a Pennsylvania Chevy dealer and racing driver. He had

to build 100 of the cars to become eligible for production-class racing, so he did—using the brand-new Corvair Corsas. Yenko offered no fewer than five stages of Stinger, each one quicker than the one before. Stingers were built mainly for the track though. If you wanted a Corvair sports car for the street, John Fitch's Sprint was the car.

Fitch has a driving record as long as Juan Fangio's, having competed over the years in every sort of race from Le Mans to SCAA regionals. When Chevrolet began treating the Corvair as an enthusiast's car in 1962, offering heavy-duty suspension, sintered metallic brake linings, and Positraction, Fitch got really interested in GM's compact. The Fitch Sprint was based on Corvair Monza coupes, though Fitch could be persuaded to work his magic on sedans, too. Its special features included quick steering, air springs, rear camber compensator, front anti-roll bar, and a special 130-hp four-carburetor engine. Exterior styling was improved with racing stripes, a vinyl-covered roof, and stone guards spread right across the front end. A wood-rimmed steering wheel and penetrating Lucas driving lights completed the package. When the restyled Corvairs appeared in 1965, Fitch built more Sprints. These were easily identifiable by an extended rear roofline in a fastback that wrapped around the rear window. Fitch disregarded the 1965-66 turbocharged 180-hp factory engine and tweaked the 140-hp mill with his usual four-carburetor setup. In this way, he achieved about 155-160 hp. Never throughout its history did a complete Sprint cost more than $3,500. It was a remarkable car, able to run circles around "normal" sports cars like the MGA and MGB. It may not have been the track star that Yenko's Stinger was—but it was every inch a sports car, and it held four people.

Sprints are expensive today, and prices are climbing all the time. A huge, enthusiastic Corvair Society exists, and Sprint parts are still obtainable. Of all the cars in this book, the Fitch Sprint is probably the most practical collector proposition. It's fun to drive, gratifyingly uncommon, and still priced well under the more exotic American sports cars, An expenditure of $5,000 should net you one of the best in the country.

PACKARD

Packard Motor Car Co.,
Detroit, Michigan

Packard built two sporting automobiles in the mid-1950s, but neither became production cars. Like Cadillac, Packard had a market of high-income buyers. Small sports cars, therefore, did not seem to be an attractive sales proposition. When a few hundred requests came in for a production version of the 1952 Pan American, Packard was as surprised as anyone.

The Pan American originated with a suggestion by the Henney Motor Company (Packard's commercial body builder) that a custom sports car be prepared for the Spring 1952 round of automobile shows. The Packard people needed an image builder at the time, so the project was commissioned. Henney designer Richard Arbib created the Pan American by chopping and channeling a stock convertible body, and shortening its wheelbase. The car was strictly a two- or three-seater: there was no back seat. The lines were smooth, and there was no chrome decoration along the body sides. Wire wheels, a continental tire, and a customized grille in the familiar Packard ox-yoke shape were the Pan Am's most notable exterior features. Power came from the 327 cubic-inch Packard straight-eight engine, hot rodded to 185 horsepower via four-barrel carburetor and high-compression head. The car was displayed at the New York International Motor Sports Show in March 1952. There it won an award for design and engineering.

Henney suggested that the Pan Am be put into production on a limited basis, and he built five more. But the project was soon abandoned. Each car cost Packard over $9,000, and would have had to be sold for at least $18,000 in the quantities contemplated.

This was enough to convince Packard that the Pan American wasn't worth the effort. However, the car influenced Packard stylist Richard A. Teague in his creation of the limited-production 1953 Caribbean.

Teague also styled the second Packard sports car, the 1954 Panther Daytona. Initially christened the Gray Wolf II, after a legendary Packard racing car of the early 1900s, the Panther was a long, swoopy-looking fiberglass roadster that rode a 122-inch wheelbase. It used standard Packard suspension and Ultramatic Drive. Its 359 cubic-inch engine developed 275 horsepower with the help of a McCulloch centrifugal supercharger.

The Panther body was clean, with a long, heavy side crease and a wrapped windshield. Its tapered rear fenders blended nicely into 1954 Clipper taillights. The front end was a bit busy: its ox-yoke grille cavity comprised an egg-crate mesh and broad front bumper. In all, Packard built five Panthers, two of which were later transformed into 1955-style models with "cathedral" taillights and an even busier front end. The original 1954 styling won *Motorsport* magazine's Merit Award and took a third place prize at the 1954 New York show. At least three Panthers still exist in the hands of collectors.

According to Teague, the Panther was never taken seriously and no volume production was discussed. But it did prove the basic worth of the big Packard straight-eight engine. At Daytona Beach in 1954, with no modifications other than a racing windshield, the Panther clocked 131.1 mph over the flying mile—the highest speed ever recorded by a car in its class.

1952 Packard Pan American

1954 Packard Panther Daytona

AC COBRA

AC Cars Ltd., Thames Ditton, Surrey, England.
Shelby-American, Inc., Santa Fe Springs, Venice,
Los Angeles, California.

We're going to be very calm about this, at least in the beginning, because there has been enough hyperbole on the subject. Nevertheless, we have to say that the great Shelby Cobras were the ultimate street sports cars. A reasonably tuned 289 Cobra will do 0 to 100 mph in 14 seconds. A 427 will do 0 to 100 to 0 in the same amount of time. The experience may devastate you. It may also spoil your appreciation for all lesser cars.

The Cobra's creator is Carroll Shelby, one-time truck driver, one-time chicken farmer, one-time Le Mans winner, a gentlemen and a sportsman: the most famous American car builder of the 1960s. Shelby had to retire from racing in 1960 because of heart trouble. But he rented space in Dean Moon's Speed Shop in Santa Fe Springs, California, and though he couldn't race cars anymore, he knew he could still build them. He had an idea which, though not new, nevertheless resulted in one of the all-time great automobiles: a potent American V8 mated to a British roadster body and chassis. The Cobra bore the AC marque, but it was a genuine hybrid: AC built the bodies and chassis, then shipped cars to California, where Shelby-American inserted the small-block, thin-wall Ford V8.

The old-line firm of AC Cars (the "AC" is short for "Autocarriers") had been building motor vehicles since 1908, and Aces since 1953. The Ace body design, by John Tojeiro, was based on the lovely Tipo 166 Ferrari Barchetta—a smooth, flowing roadster with rounded tail and an aggressive, blunt grille. A rudimentary soft top and side curtains were provided, but ACs were meant to be driven without a top.

To Shelby, the most important item was the Ace's granite-strong tubular chassis. It used four-wheel independent suspension, including tubular lower wishbones and transverse leaf springs. Its optional 2-liter Bristol four made it quick; the light, powerful Ford V8 transformed it into a tiger. Shelby talked Ford into shipping him a pair of small-block V8s, and persuaded AC to send over an Ace. He cleaned up the Ace by making changes in styling details, and by slightly extending the nose. AC was pleased, since Bristol no longer supplied 2-liter engines. Ford cooperated because Lee Iacocca, then Ford Division head, wanted to reap publicity from Ford-backed racing efforts.

In Cobras, the Ford V8 initially displaced 260 cubic

1965 Cobra

inches. After the first 75 were built, Shelby changed to the 289-cid engine which developed 271 hp. The work continued, all the way to 380 horsepower with four Weber carburetors, reworked heads, and a full-race camshaft. The AC steering was improved by a Shelby-designed rack-and-pinion system. The base Cobra sold for $5,995, only slightly more than a Corvette. Shelby's object was to beat Ferrari and Corvette on every sort of track from SCCA to Le Mans, and he did so. But he also created a magnificent street sports car in the process. Its interior was Spartan, its weather protection meager, and its capacity limited by a 90-inch wheelbase. But the Cobra's lines were pure and lovely; and Corvette, Ferrari, Jaguar, and Aston Martin could not touch it on any kind of road.

Shelby received assistance from Pete Brock, a former designer of the Sting Ray; and Ken Miles and Phil Remington, recently of the Reventlow-Scarab organization. Sanctioned-class racing Cobras first appeared in 1963. Bob Johnson won the SCCA A-Production championship in a Cobra that year; Bob Holbert captured the manufacturers division of the U.S. Road Race of Champions. Cobra 289s could not beat the light racing Corvette Grand Sports at Nassau that winter, but after 1964, Cobras owned the SCCA.

Back in California, during the winter of 1963-64, Brock conjured up the Kamm-backed Cobra Daytona coupes. These ran 1-2-3-5-7 in class at Sebring, and fourth overall at Le Mans. Cobras kept running and winning through 1966, but by then Shelby had stopped building 289s. AC continued with 27 cars using 289 V8s in the 427 body. Then Shelby hatched the mighty 427 Cobra.

The 427 is so alien in performance from the other cars in this book that it really belongs in a chapter by itself. That 0-100-0 figure of 14 seconds must be emphasized. Bear in mind that in 1964 an Aston Martin performed the same feat in 25 seconds, and you'll have a rough idea of the explosive performance offered by this brute of an automobile. Figures for straight acceleration are astonishing: 0-60 in 4.5 seconds or less; 0-100 in 8.7. A 427 can put even the most experienced driver to the test. It had a stronger frame than the 289, coils instead of leaf springs, and much fatter tires. But that's irrelevant to all but the top 0.1 percent of the world's drivers. The 427 is a demon, a dangerous car for the overconfident motorist. In the wrong hands, it can be lethal.

For all these reasons, the Cobra 427 is the most desirable American sports car ever produced. In 1967 you could buy one for $6,000. Today it takes at least $40,000, and the cars have been advertised for well above that. Quantities are limited: only 356 were built. The 427 can exceed the 55 mph speed limit by half in first gear. Therefore, we recommend it only to those drivers who'll settle for nothing less than the most violent sports car. And to them, price is no object.

For the rest of us, forced to choose between the 427 and the 289 (there are about 50,000 people who would like that choice), the smaller-engined Cobra is the obvious selection. It doesn't handle as well as the 427; it is less sophisticated; and it takes perhaps a fifth less effort to steer, handle, and brake. But the 289 really is a wonderful car to drive—lightning quick, and responsive in the hands of good drivers. Since 855 of the 289s were built, counting the AC overseas versions, they are easier to obtain than the 427s. Today, it costs perhaps $20,000 to $30,000 to own the 289. And like the 427, in its own sphere, the 289 will continue to appreciate each year as we pass from the age of Carroll Shelby and his sinfully wasteful, brutally powerful, magnificent Cobras.

1966 Cobra 427

FOREIGN BODIES-AMERICAN MUSCLE: ALLARD

ALLARD

**Allard Motor Co. Ltd., Clapham,
London, England**

When sports-car people mention a car that looks as if it's been hammered together by a blacksmith, they are usually talking about an Allard. Sidney Allard's cars were not pretty. Their crude construction was comparable to that of a Warwickshire farm plow. But they were incredibly effective. It took a lot of courage to squirrel a J2 around a road course; to spectators the thing resembled a bucket of heavy iron objects flying in various directions along a generally forward course. But the J2 was so fast in a straight line that its looks didn't matter. Fitted with a V8 from a monster Cadillac, Chrysler or Olds, the J2 was the world's fastest street sports car in its heyday, the Cobra of the early 1950s.

Sidney Allard began bolting cars together in 1936, using Ford V8 and Lincoln Zephyr V-12 engines. They were quite successful in Britain, especially in the muddy trials competition that was so popular there. After the war, Allard was given a simple assignment by the government: build a car that could be exchanged for American dollars. In turn, the government would not cut off his supply of steel. Allard obliged by building cars that could accept American engines from flathead Mercury V8s to big-inch Cadillacs. Allard built sedans, tourers and coupes, and the Type J sports car. Typically, the J was a low-slung, mean-looking brute with cycle fenders, cut-down doors, a tiny flip-up racing windshield, and a plethora of bulges, louvers, scoops and buckles. The cockpit was spare, but all business. An aluminum dash housed a set of big, white-on-black instruments, including a tach redlined at around 5500 rpm, and a speedometer reading up to 150 mph.

The first J-series car, the J1, had a De Dion rear axle and a queer transverse-leaf front suspension. This was independent in theory, but a split-beam axle in fact. The car was fast, but dicey on racetracks and less agile than the Jaguar XK-120. In 1951, early in the run of successor J2 models, Allard switched to new front-end geometry and coil springs, which improved the J2's grip immensely. This put Allard squarely in the midst of the competition, and assured its racing successes until the arrival of the even more sophisticated second-generation Jaguar and Ferrari models.

The ultimate Allard, though, was the J2X, introduced in 1951. The weight distribution on its 100-inch wheelbase was improved over previous models. Fitted with a Cadillac or Chrysler engine, this machine was a virtual tornado. It would leap from 0 to 100 mph in 12 seconds (just 3 seconds slower than the 427 Cobra that would appear 16 years later). Top speed varied according to the rear axles fitted. With the 3.20:1 ratio, the top speed was somewhere around 140 mph. Steering was quick and suprisingly responsive. The J2X plowed a bit in the corners, but drivers Erwin Goldschmidt and Fred Wacker fearlessly flung them into all kinds of corners with remarkable effectiveness. A J2X storming through a 90-mph bend was not very sophisticated, but it usually stayed far ahead of its rivals.

A good J2 sells for around $15,000 today; J2Xs cost more than that. They don't come up for sale often, because their owners are among the most satisfied collectors in the world.

Type J Allard with split front axle

The 140-mph J2X

BRISTOL

Bristol Cars Ltd., Filton, Bristol, England

The Bristol Aeroplane Company began building automobiles in 1947, and Bristol Cars is still doing so. Bristols became hybrids in 1961, when the six-cylinder 100D2 engine was abandoned in favor of a 313 cubic-inch Chrysler V8 which provided 250 horsepower. This was the Bristol Type 407; successive models spanned Types 408 through 411. Bristol's current offerings are still Chrysler-powered. The 412 convertible and 603 coupe sell for a stratospheric $60,000 in Britain.

The essence of a Bristol is luxury, refinement, and aircraft standards of construction. Although their V8 engines shared Allard's American character, the Bristols were really the antithesis of a J2X. The majority of Bristols were coupes, fitted with TorqueFlite automatic transmission, leather upholstery, polished walnut, and wool carpeting.

The basis of the Type 407 was a four-place coupe with a 114-inch wheelbase built for Bristol by Jones Brothers of Willesden, London. It was roomy, and had clean lines, a capacious trunk, and a long hood which ended in a rectangular grille cavity. Hollowed out front fenders, (housing a spare tire on one side, tools and batteries on the other), carried over from previous six-cylinder models. They are still present on modern examples. A panel hinged at the creaseline two-thirds of the way up the fender permitted access to the cavity. The 407 would do 0 to 100 mph in 26 seconds, and had a top speed of over 125 mph. Its stiff and extremely strong box-section girder frame was virtually unbreakable. True to Bristol's aircraft heritage, the car's fuel tank was positioned far ahead of the trunk, and was protected on all sides by steel girders. Ironically, importation of Bristol cars to the States ended when the company failed to meet U. S. safety regulations after 1967.

The 1964-65 Type 408 was given a high, blunt nose, a horizontal-bar grille, and a flatter roof than the 407. Its only mechanical alteration was Armstrong Select-aride adjustable rear shock absorbers. The 408 Mark II switched to the 318 cubic-inch Chrysler engine and a higher rear axle ratio. These features were carried over into the 132-mph Type 409 of 1966. Both the 409 and 410, which carried Bristol into 1969, were softer-riding than their forerunners, but their handling was better thanks to improved weight distribution. On the 410, 15-inch tires replaced the previous 16-inchers, and the track was wider. Acceleration had been improved to 23 seconds for the 0-100 sprint. Braking, with Girling discs, was beyond reproach.

The early V8 Bristols were produced at a rate of three cars a week. Production totals were 300 units each for the 407 and 408; 150 for the one-year 409; and 450 for the three-year 410. Needless to say, the cars aren't cheap today. American enthusiasts have to pay more than $10,000 for a left-hand-drive model in the United States. Some have settled for right-hand-drive cars imported from Britain, where they sell for $5,000 to $7,500. American regulations prevent the importation of any Bristol made after 1967, but for those willing to settle for the earlier models there are rewards. The factory refurbishes old models and stocks body parts back to 1949. The mechanical situation, of course, is no problem to Americans.

The Bristol is more a grand tourer than a sports car. But in terms of performance, safety, luxury, and quality of construction, few automobiles surpass its combination of American power and old-world craftmanship.

1966 Bristol

DE TOMASO

De Tomaso Automobili SpA, Modena, Italy

1974 Pantera by De Tomaso

Alejandro de Tomaso was an expatriot Argentine who built formula cars and sports racers in the early 1960s, and then decided to construct a sports car to suit his own high standards. His first effort was the mid-engine Vallelunga, equipped with a 1500cc English Ford engine. It was a good car, but not terribly fast. Its successor was the ultimate De Tomaso: the magnificent Mangusta. Designed by Giorgio Giugiaro, the most talented automobile stylist of the day, the Mangusta was one of those rare machines that is perfect from every angle. A low, svelte bullet of a car, it seems to get better the more you look at it. A 289 cubic-inch Ford V8, mounted behind the driver, powered the Mangusta. The car was equipped with a five-speed ZF transaxle, a limited-slip differential, and Girling disc brakes at all four wheels. As fast as it was beautiful, the Mangusta would do 155 mph. Racing-car design even influenced its wheels: the rear ones were larger than those in the front. A Mangusta, complete with air conditioning, sold for only about $11,000 after delivery to the United States. Today, of course, the price is more than double that.

By 1970, Alejandro de Tomaso had acquired two coachbuilding firms, Ghia and Vignale. These companies tempted Ford stylists, whose ideas took the form of lifeless clay models; in Italy, stylists cut their prototypes out of sheet steel with tin snips. Ford bought De Tomaso Automobili, fed Ghia and Vignale into its designing echelon, and reworked the Mangusta.

The result was the De Tomaso Pantera, which was nearly as pretty as the Mangusta and $1,000 less expensive. It retained the best Mangusta features such as the mid-mounted engine, ZF transaxle, disc brakes, all-independent suspension and unit body-chassis. But its larger 351-cid V8 produced 310 horsepower and gave the Pantera a top speed alleged to be 162 mph.

There were two difficulties, though. In U.S. crash tests, the first Panteras exploded when they rammed the cement barrier. Ford sent them back to be redesigned. In 1974 federal bumper standards finished them off as production sports cars. A total of 5,269 had been built and were sold before this. With the demise of the Pantera, Alejandro de Tomaso sold his interest to Ford.

Panteras can be obtained through Lincoln-Mercury dealers, but most would rather you didn't show up with one for service. De Tomaso's electrical system is faulty, the car overheats, and occasionally it falls apart. Ford partially rebuilt most Panteras at vast expense and put them under its warranty. Today, a large Pantera club provides assistance to owners. Because so many Panteras were produced, prices have remained stable. A good one today will cost $12,000 to $15,000. This may sound pretty high, but really is not compared to similar models. The Pantera is the cheapest dart-shaped, mid-engined, 150-mph super-car you can get these days—and the only one you can find for $12,000.

JENSEN

**Jensen Motors Ltd., West Bromwich,
Staffordshire, England**

Jensen Interceptor III

The Jensen brothers, Richard and Allen, like Sidney Allard, built Anglo-American sports-car hybrids with huge V8 engines bolted to conventional chassis and quintessential British sports bodies. But Jensen cars, beginning with the 1963 CV8, were far more luxurious than Allards. They were big, roomy sports cars capable of covering great distances at more than 100 mph, running quietly and smoothly.

Jensen's first cars, built in the 1930s, were powered by a Ford V8. After the war Jensen switched to domestic power plants like the Austin A.135, a 4-liter six. But the Jensens hoped for better performance and turned again to Detroit for an engine. Eventually they made a deal with Chrysler for the 354 and 383 cubic-inch wedge-head V8s, which developed 330 horsepower. The Jensen CV8, driven by these engines, was a fiberglass coupe with a curb weight of only 3,500 pounds. In average tune, the car could do 130 mph. It could run up to 60 in about eight seconds, clock the quarter mile in 16 seconds, and deliver fuel mileage of around 15 mpg.

The trouble with the CV8 was that is was perhaps the ugliest car in the world. Its front end sprouted diagonally arranged quad headlights set into big oval cutouts, a hood scoop, a splashy Jensen badge, and a funny little turned-down grille. The CV8 had a face only the Jensen brothers could love. Its price, twice that of the best Corvette you could buy, made it impossible to

sell in the United States. When it was phased out in early 1966, few shed tears.

At that point the Jensens made a wise decision. They retained all the good features of the CV8—Chrysler engine, robust chassis, high-quality construction—but they replaced the homely fiberglass body. The new design was by Vignale. It was a clean-lined steel coupe, with a greenhouse not unlike Studebaker's Avanti. Named Interceptor, the new Jensen performed as well as its predecessor, had acceptable if not sensational looks, and sold for just a few dollars more. It was vastly more popular, and was produced through 1972. An intriguing offshoot was the Interceptor FF. This car, like the CV8, featured Ferguson-type hypoid final drive to all four wheels. Jensen stopped production of the Interceptor and its FF variation in 1973. The company sought greater volume with the Lotus-powered Jensen-Healey two-seater.

Jensen's exports to this country were sporadic at best, and federal regulations after 1968 prevented all but a handful of Interceptors from arriving here. As with Bristol, models built after 1967 cannot be obtained without a lot of expensive modification. CV8s are more common than Interceptors, but you would have to be a rabid Jensen enthusiast to appreciate their styling. The FF versions are technically interesting, and will probably prove to be the most valuable Jensen collectors' items 20 or 30 years from now.

Organizations

AC Owners Club, American Centre, 88 Cushing Street, Hingham, MA 02043.

Allard Register, 8 Paget Close, Horsham, West Sussex, RH13 6HD, England.

AMX: Classic AMX Club International, 5731 Walker Avenue, Loves Park, IL 61111.

Apollo Register, 9607 West Bexhill Drive, Kensington, MD 20795.

Arnolt-Bristol Owners Club, 3900 Langley Road, Charlotte, NC 28215.

Bristol Owners Club, 5 St. Leonard's Court, East Sheen, London S.W.14, England.

Buick Club of America, Post Office Box 853, Garden Grove, CA 92642.

Chrysler: Walter P. Chrysler Club, Post Office Box 4705, North Hollywood, CA 91607.

Corvair Society of America (CORSA), Post Office Box 2488, Pensacola, FL 32503.

Corvette: National Corvette Restorers Club, Post Office Box 34377, Omaha, NB 68134.

Crosley Automobile Club, 200 Ridge Road East, Williamson, NY 14589.

Cunningham Museum Associates, 250 Baker Street, Costa Mesa, CA 92626.

De Tomaso: Pantera International, 1775 South Alvira Street, Los Angeles, CA 90035.

Devin: The Devin Register, Post Office Box 18, Nyack, NY 10960.

Dodge: Walter P. Chrysler Club, Post Office Box 4705, North Hollywood, CA 91607.

Ford: Classic T-Bird Club International, Post Office Box 2398, Culver City, CA 90230.

Jensen Owners Club, 63 Northlands Avenue, Orpington, Kent, England.

Kaiser-Darrin: K-F Owners Club, 157 Black Canyon Stage, Phoenix, AZ 85020.

Mercer Associates, c/o Prof. Cain, Business Admin. Dept., Texas Tech, Lubbock, TX 79409.

Miamisburg Crosley Car Club, 829 E. Cottage Avenue, Miamisburg, OH 45342.

Nash-Healey Car Club, 100 Church Street, Lakeland, GA 31635.

Packard Automobile Classics, Post Office Box 2808, Oakland, CA 94618.

Pontiac-Oakland Club International, 3298 Maple Avenue, Allegany, NY 14706.

Shelby-American Automobile Club, 24-C April Lane, Norwalk, CT 06850.

Stutz Nuts, C. McCord Purdy, 3856 Arthington Boulevard, Indianapolis, IN 46226.

Sunbeam Owners Club, 43 Terrace Avenue, Ossining, NY 10562.

Sunbeam Tiger Owners Association, 5067 Valley Park Avenue, Fremont, CA 94538.

Publications

AC
Kopec, Rick. *Shelby American Guide.* Shelby-American Automobile Club Inc., 415 Dorchester Avenue, Reading, PA 19609.

Allard
Lush, Tom. *Allard, The Inside Story.* Classic Motorbooks, Post Office Box 2, Osceola, WI 54020.

Bristol
Setright, L.J.K. *Bristol Cars and Engines.* Classic Motorbooks, Post Office Box 2, Osceola, WI 54020.

Buick
Norbye, Jan P.; Dunne, Jim. *Buick, The Postwar Years.* Classic Motorbooks, Post Office Box 2, Osceola, WI 54020.

Cadillac
Hendry, Maurice D. *Cadillac, The Complete History.* Automobile Quarterly Publications, 245 West Main Street, Kutztown, PA 19530.

Chrysler
Langworth, Richard M. *Chrysler, The Postwar Years.* Dragonwyck Publishing Ltd., Burrage Road, Contoocook, NH 03229.

Corvair
Ludvigsen, Karl E. *Corvair.* Automobile Quarterly Publications, 245 West Main Street, Kutztown, PA 19530.

Cunningham
Car Classics. Dragonwyck Publishing Ltd., Burrage Road, Contoocook, NH 03229.

DeSoto-Plymouth
Butler, Don E. *DeSoto-Plymouth Story.* Crestline Publishing, 1251 North Jefferson Avenue, Sarasota, FL 33577.

Dodge
MacPherson, Thomas. *Dodge Story.* Crestline Publishing, 1251 North Jefferson Avenue, Sarasota, FL 33577.

Dual-Ghia, Edwards, Kurtis/Muntz, Woodill
Special-Interest Autos. Special-Interest Autos Magazine, Post Office Box 196, Bennington, VT 05201.

Excalibur, Kaiser-Darrin
Langworth, Richard M. *Kaiser-Frazer.* Dragonwyck Publishing Ltd., Burrage Road, Contoocook, NH 03229.

Ford
Miller, Ray. *Thunderbird.* Evergreen Press, Post Office Box 1711, Oceanside, CA 92054.

Gaylord, Nash-Healey, Stutz
Automobile Quarterly. Automobile Quarterly Publications, 245 West Main Street, Kutztown, PA 19530.

Packard
Martin, Terry; Bradley, James; Langworth, Richard M.; Weber, Don; Yost, Morgan; Phillips, Richard; Leslie, C.A.; Hamlin, George; Heinmuller, Dwight. *Packard.* Automobile Quarterly Publications, 245 West Main Street, Kutztown, PA 19530.

Pontiac
Norbye, Jan P.; Dunn, Jim. *Pontiac, The Postwar Years.* Classic Motorbooks, Post Office Box 2, Osceola, WI 54020.

Shelby
Kopec, Rick. *Shelby-American Guide.* Shelby-American Automobile Club Inc., 415 Dorchester Avenue, Reading, PA 19609.

Sunbeam
Kopec, Rick. *Shelby American Guide.* Shelby-American Automobile Club Inc., 415 Dorchester Avenue, Reading, PA 19609.